THE 2-HOUR TUTOR

How to replace your 60h per week teaching job with a 2h per week tuition business

ELLIE BAKER

Does this sound familiar?

"I've tried starting a tuition business but I have no idea how to market myself. I've tried posting on social media but it's just not working."

"I'm rubbish at marketing - I'm just no good at selling myself. It makes me cringe!"

"If this doesn't start working soon, I'll have to go back and get another teaching job."

"Everyone I speak to just wants 1:1 tuition. How do I convince them that a group programme is better for their kids?"

"I'm worried that niching will result in less clients. I can't afford to turn people away!"

"I'm at full capacity with 1:1. How can I earn more without adding more hours to my plate?"

"Local tutors all seem to charge £30-£40 per hour. How can I charge more?"

Praise for Ellie Baker

"I am about halfway through Ellie's amazing programme. I have spent £1000s on other trainings and all that did was make other coaches rich! This feels totally different. I feel totally supported. I love the community we have and seeing other people's successes spurs me on. This time it feels different. This time my ADHD brain has a step-by-step process to follow and I am excited about the business I am building! Thank you, Ellie, Mel and Terry."

Jean Ramsay, former secondary teacher

"Ellie is a TOP educational business coach whose programme has been inspirational and life-changing. After teaching for thirty years, I have now left the classroom and am about halfway through building my own GCSE fast-track programme, which I'm feeling very confident about. I'm looking forward to moving from tutoring 1-2-1 to my group programme, which promises to be more effective for the students and a more sustainable income for me. I highly recommend Ellie's programme. It is superb."

Claire Davidson, founder of The English Lab

"I am about halfway through my time with Ellie and to say it has been transformational would be an understatement. From day 1 I have been challenged to change my way of thinking and encouraged to truly explore my potential. Alongside the personal development, I have also grown as an entrepreneur and developed a wide range of marketing skills that are starting to pay dividends. Although I have not completed the course, I have already signed up 2 students to my high-ticket programme and I have a long list of leads that I am working on as we speak. If you are in any doubt about working with Ellie, I would be happy to speak to you about my experiences."

Ross, Head of Sixth Form

"The course is so much more than what I originally thought it would be. It has taught me things I didn't even realise I needed to learn. Ellie and her team are great, they are so supportive and the modules are set out in an easy to follow and structured way. I'm so happy that I signed up to this, it is fully worth every penny of my investment."

Nikki Collins, Maths Tutor

"From the start, it is clear that Ellie has designed her course thoughtfully and compassionately.

Leaving a teaching career (which I thought was for life) in order to set up a business is a big change. Ellie has been there in the classroom and is now a successful business woman so she can relate very well to others in the same situation.

In the space of a few months, I have learned a great deal about owning a business and have felt supported along the way not only by Ellie but also by her colleagues: Mel & Terry.

The self-study element is great as it fits nicely around other commitments (even if you're still working) and I have really enjoyed getting to know other people on the course. It's wonderful to have a little community of people going through the same process - we have been able to help each other out along the way. For me, this was invaluable.

I feel the course is well worth the financial investment. Signing up with Ellie was the start of a huge new chapter in my life!"

Jen Bromley, 11+ Tutor

"Ellie really helped me at a time in my teaching career when I needed it most. Having been an unhappy secondary school teacher for several years (jumping through hoops, struggling to manage with my work/life balance and constantly feeling under pressure, overworked and under-valued) I needed a change.

She helped me with my low self-esteem and developed my escape plan.

I now have the confidence and toolkit to move forward with my new business venture knowing I'll never have to worry about the stress of marking, target setting and exam preparation again...priceless!

Thank you so much!"

Elizabeth May - former primary teacher

"I found Ellie as I was coming up to my 20th year in education; teaching full time as a primary school teacher and Phase Leader. I was highly regarded, respected and outwardly doing a great job but inside I was drowning, exhausted, anxious, depressed and knew I couldn't continue till retirement that way. Ellie taught me the skills to launch my business and take my next step - out of the classroom! Thank you Ellie"

Martha Kilner - former primary teacher

"Joining Ellie's programme has been truly life changing! Ellie covers absolutely every aspect of starting and maintaining an online business, and even helps you to generate ideas if you're stuck! I have a new confidence and optimism for my business and I'm so grateful to Ellie for all her help and expertise over the last 12 weeks."

Tami Darias - former MFL teacher

"I found Ellie's course at quite a significant time in my life. I was going through treatment for breast cancer and had decided now was the time to put my health and happiness first. I had been looking for an exit strategy from the classroom for quite a while as I was demoralised by our education system and never-ending government interventions and cut-backs. I didn't know how I could continue without the skills and confidence to try something new. I was definitely institutionalised! Ellie showed me there was an alternative to the classroom that I was more than capable of doing. She gave me the confidence and belief that I could do it and supported me emotionally. Ellie is a lovely, caring person that wants the best for teachers. She has been there and knows exactly what we are going through. She held my hand through the whole process which is just what I needed. I have now handed in my notice and feel like a weight has been lifted. I have all the skills to grow my business and am really excited about the future. Thank you, Ellie, for all your help."

Alison Conolly - former primary teacher turned maths tutor

"Thank you, Ellie & Terry, – this has been a life-changing decision!! I will forever be thankful to you both. It's been quite a journey but your support has been invaluable and I wouldn't be where I am today without you. keep on doing what you do, it's such important work!"

Jayne Curran

"I've just completed the Happy and Free Teacher Academy and I can honestly say it's been life changing. Ellie gives clear, actionable advice every step of the way which has allowed me to build my own business with minimal confusion and stress. I can also say that she's one of the most lovely people I've ever worked with. I chose the self-study option and booked a 1:1 call later when I started to have more specific questions and Ellie was fantastic. She talked me through what I was struggling with and after just 1 hour, I knew exactly what to do next and how to do it. I'm now very excited to be joining her Alumni group and continuing on this journey. Thank you so much, Ellie!"

Jen Shaw

"I have recently completed the 2-Hour Tutor programme and I would highly recommend the course to anyone who is serious about leaving teaching. It is thoughtfully planned out and Ellie is an encouraging and reassuring mentor. The support from Terry and Mel has also been invaluable - from mindset coaching, wording of key documents and IT support! Thank you all so much!"

Angela Beckett - former primary teacher

We do not give any warranty regarding earnings or income. There is no guarantee that you will earn any money purely through our methods. Examples in this book are not to be interpreted as a promise or guarantee of earnings.

The 2-HOUR TUTOR
First edition (2023)

Copyright © 2023 Ellie Baker

All rights reserved.

No part of this book may be reproduced, or stored in a retrieval system, or transmitted in any form or by any means, electronic, mechanical, photocopying, recording, or otherwise, without the prior written permission of the copyright owner, except for the use of brief quotations embodied in articles and reviews.

Cover by: SyrendipityDesign

To all the teachers, tutors and children's activity providers out there making a difference to children's lives. You are the unsung superheroes of our society. I thank you.

Foreword by Terry Hill
Business Psychologist and Best-Selling Author

To the reader

I'm the Proud Dad here, so excited about what Ellie has created. Also the dad that advised her to give teaching a miss based on my own brief but painful experience. Fortunately, Ellie wasn't deterred and she quickly exceeded my expectations. But the frustrations that come with the job soon mounted. So many teachers simply "cannot carry on" but neither can they contemplate leaving! They need to find new ways to make a difference, to explore life beyond the classroom, but how?

Now Ellie has turned her considerable experience and expertise into a purpose, a proven pathway to independence and success that others can follow. Here's an amazing manual for you, the reader, with all the tips and tools for building that new future. So much value has been packed into such a short book.

So, can you make the change? With this book it's a definite yes! You already have so many transferable skills having done one of the hardest jobs around. So many valued abilities and experiences you can pack for your journey. And it's such a rewarding journey, with Ellie at your side, guiding and supporting you all the way. She understands your frustrations, your need to make the impact you choose, how to keep your independence and build your chosen lifestyle. Ellie highlights the inevitable fears you will have on the way, why they happen most to those who continue to grow and flourish and most importantly how to handle these. The toolkit for success is all here.

So, have you been a mere spectator of life outside the classroom? Too involved with your duties to think of your own needs? Instead of looking through a window why not try a mirror, one that reveals your innermost strengths and passions. Use this book to find that new purpose and start that journey.

You will surprise yourself. Better get packing!

Terry

Preface

Dear teacher,

As you hold this book in your hands, it's likely that you have walked the hallways of schools or are still immersed in the vibrant world of teaching. If that's the case, you won't be surprised when I touch upon the topic of our education system and its flaws, along with the call for change.

Now, you might be thinking, "Why would you want to entice teachers away from their roles, leaving the ship to sink even further?" But rest assured, that's not my intention here. I want to clarify that my purpose is not to lure happy teachers away, but rather to shed light on a different path for those who feel disheartened and stuck within the system.

Passion for helping young people runs deep within us, and that's incredible! However, we also recognize that passion alone cannot mend all the cracks in the system's hull.

Having been a teacher within the system, I tried my best to make positive changes from the inside. But as time went on, I realised that some challenges were beyond my reach from that perspective. I knew I had to find another way to make a difference.

Remember the saying, "It takes a village to raise a child"? Well, I believe it takes an army of empowered teachers to bring about lasting change. By stepping away from the system, we can gain fresh perspectives and be better equipped to create meaningful transformations for ourselves and our students.

So, my mission with this book is to free educators who yearn for a better way—one that liberates them from the shackles of rigid systems and empowers them to make changes with integrity, authenticity, and yes, a healthy dose of joy!

Now, you might wonder why I deem myself qualified to guide you on this journey. While I have been on the 'educational business' path for more than a decade now, truth be told, I don't have any formal business or marketing credentials. My official coaching qualification came from an online course I took during lockdown, but in reality, it started in my early teens when my dad gifted me my first personal growth book; 'Unleash The Power Within' by Tony Robbins. The rest is history!

Given that you are reading this book, you're likely in one of two places:

- You're seriously considering quitting your teaching job and you've got your eyes on the next step – a tutoring business

OR

- You've already quit your teaching job, but you're stuck in the feast or famine cycle with your 1:1 tuition and you're interested in phasing this out in favour of more streamlined approach.

Either way – that's what this book will help you with.

In this book you will learn why group tuition programmes are the best way to deliver an incredible result for your students, whilst freeing up your time and making more money (even while you're on holiday)!

With the right structure and marketing strategy, you can enrol new students every month without ever needing to worry about squeezing in even more 1:1 tuition, or not being paid during school holidays

Read on if you want to come into my world and learn about:

- The "2-Hour-a-Week" Group Programme Structure that frees up your time to serve as many people as you like.

- Releasing your fears about leaving teaching or charging more for tuition. Feel empowered and understand that it's NOT YOUR FAULT - the education system is flawed, not you.

- Understanding and knowing your true self again - what are your values and passions? What gives you joy?

- How to decide on an online course you would love to create for one type of audience. No more planning 20 lessons per week.

- How to create, market and sell your course - replace & exceed your teaching income.

So, let's discover the possibilities beyond the classroom walls and unleash the empowered teacher within ourselves. Together, we can create a wave of positive change, not just for our students, but for the entire education landscape. Get ready for an adventure that will inspire and empower you in ways you never imagined!

Contents

Introduction		1
Chapter 1	The problem teachers face	4
Chapter 2	My story	8
Chapter 3	The solution	11
Chapter 4	'Unschool' your mind	15
Chapter 5	The Happy and Free Success Mindset	20
Chapter 6	Time to clear the decks	25
Chapter 7	Habits for success	30
Chapter 8	Letting go compassionately	38
Chapter 9	Feel the Fear	43
Chapter 10	Deciding on your ideal programme	47
Chapter 11	Bold Beliefs	57
Chapter 12	Money	62
Chapter 13	Choose your niche	82
Chapter 14	Cracking content	94
Chapter 15	Review and Practicalities to consider	98
Chapter 16	Tech and social media	105
Chapter 17	The non-salesy seller mindset	124
Chapter 18	Making it Happen	131
Final words		138
Bibliography		146
About the Author		147
Acknowledgements		148
Contact Ellie		150

Introduction

"Please don't become a teacher," my dad begged me back in 2003. He'd been there and done that, and had since made his exit and carved a niche for himself as a corporate coach. At the time, I was contemplating leaving my new role as a sales rep for a pharmaceutical firm in the UK. I couldn't help but wonder why I should leave behind all the perks - a company car, laptop, phone, decent salary, bonuses, and fancy trips - and exchange it for an £18,000 annual salary as a newly qualified teacher (preceded by a small bursary for my training to last me for the next 12 months).

But for me, it all boiled down to a deep need to make a difference. I know it might sound cheesy and clichéd, but if you're reading this, you probably get it too. Maybe you were in another role before becoming a teacher, or perhaps you always knew teaching was your calling. For me, I couldn't justify studying languages for four years at university and then doing something unrelated. I believed in the value of transferring my passion for the subject to young minds, teaching them to broaden their horizons and experience life beyond the UK.

So, at the age of 23, I embarked on my PGCE at Derby University. From the very first day in the classroom, I realised teaching was a tough gig. Gone were the comforts of my previous luxury life! Instead, I found myself regularly walking home with my Asda shopping, drenched, after my clapped-out Astra had broken down, yet again.

Despite the challenges, I stuck with it and qualified as a teacher. I then left the Midlands for Leeds to join my now husband Gareth, who had just started his corporate career as a Chartered Surveyor. I got my first paid role as a secondary MFL teacher at a school in Pontefract, and that's when my roller-coaster journey truly began.

It was more rewarding than anything I had ever done before, yet more soul-crushing at the same time. I soon realised that the problem wasn't just with my current school; the whole system was deeply flawed. Over the ten years I spent as a school teacher, I witnessed staff bullying and all sorts of toxic behaviours that went against everything I believed in. But amidst all that, I participated and ran fantastic trips for kids and I met some truly dedicated and wonderful people and (yes), some narcissistic ones too.

I was privileged to help thousands of children broaden their horizons and create a better future for themselves. It was a wild, bumpy, challenging, beautiful, terrifying and wonderful ride that I don't regret for one moment. However, it was also completely unsustainable.

This is not a memoir of my teaching career; that can wait for another book. Instead, I'm looking back on the milestone of being a teacher for ten years and now an educational business owner for the same duration. Nowadays, I help teachers and tutors, like you, break free from the constraints of the education system and turn your passion into a thriving business that not only allows you to give, but also gives back to you. Teachers are some of the most wonderful, altruistic, and kind-hearted people out there, and you deserve more from life.

This is a how-to guide to help you convert your teaching genius into a successful tutoring business that offers you both time and financial abundance. It's about gaining the freedom to make the impact you desire most.

So, without further ado… let's dive in!

Chapter 1
The problem teachers face

People often question why I exclusively work with teachers, often teachers who are also parents. The reason is clear – teachers face immense scrutiny and a significant pay gap when compared to other professions.

Teacher burnout in the UK has become a mainstream problem. This is no wonder, given the constant juggling of meaningless admin tasks, feeling disempowered when it comes to classroom management, and relentless scrutiny which is unmatched by any other profession. For more and more teachers, this is leading to 'cognitive dissonance' where they may experience a disconnect between their passion for teaching and the taxing reality of the daily grind.

Recent workforce statistics from the UK Department for Education indicate that in the 2021/2022 academic year, 39,930 teachers quit the profession for reasons unrelated to retirement.

This represents a whopping 8.8% of teachers within the profession, a five-fold increase compared to just 7,800 departures during the 2020/2021 academic year. Currently, around one in four teachers in the UK quit within their first 3 years, highlighting the urgent need for change.

The misconception that teaching is an easy job does not help matters. This erroneous belief persists because outsiders don't fully understand its demands. On top of that, schools are evaluated using soul-crushing yardsticks like OFSTED and league tables, making success feel like an uphill battle for all concerned; students included.

The demands of teaching can often leave little room for personal life, and when teachers become parents, they find themselves confronted with tough choices. One option is part-time work, which may require sacrificing income to raise their young family. On the other hand, full-time work can result in limited time with their children, causing a constant struggle to strike a balance.

Another alternative is becoming a stay-at-home parent, putting their professional aspirations on hold to focus solely on their children. Each choice involves significant sacrifices, and the realisation dawns that the career that they have painstakingly built for years may not be compatible with the demands of parenthood.

To achieve true flexibility and balance, some teachers contemplate starting their own tuition businesses. However, this decision is not without challenges, particularly due to the ingrained conditioning from the traditional education system.

Overcoming societal expectations and embracing entrepreneurship can feel daunting, but it offers the possibility of creating a better work-life balance.

Having personally experienced the challenges of balancing the roles of being both a mother and a teacher, I am committed to supporting teachers, especially women, in navigating these obstacles and establishing successful tuition businesses. I firmly believe that change begins within us, and with the right support and mindset, teachers can carve out a new path that allows them to thrive both professionally and personally.

By embracing entrepreneurship and advocating for flexibility, we can pave the way for a more inclusive and balanced future for teachers as they juggle their vital roles as educators and parents.

Leaving a 'secure job' in education may seem like a huge risk, or like you're entering unfamiliar territory, leading to feelings of uncertainty. You may also feel pressured to stay because of financial needs, lack of any other career options in other fields, or mental blocks around how to start a business of your own.

With all this going on in our heads, it's easy to see why so many teachers perpetually postpone that day when they walk out of the school gates for good.

You may feel held back by feelings of guilt when you think about leaving the classroom. This may be due to a sense that you're abandoning your students, feel like a failure or that you're giving up on a dream or identity you worked so hard to achieve.

With most teachers being true altruists, we are typically very committed to our career and leaving may feel like you are disregarding your values and calling.

However, it's not only teachers who are opting out of the system. An increasing number of parents in the UK are choosing to withdraw their children from traditional schooling, with reasons including concerns about the quality of education, standardised testing pressures, misalignment with more gentle parenting approaches and a desire for more personalised and flexible learning experiences. Educational approaches such as homeschooling, unschooling, and Montessori education are increasingly popular, with many parents believing they better cater to their children's individual needs and interests.

Additionally, the COVID-19 pandemic has accelerated the adoption of online learning and remote education, providing parents and carers with more options for tailored and home-based education. As a result, this shift away from the conventional education system reflects a growing demand for educational alternatives that better suit the diverse needs and aspirations of today's families. In short, there are children and families out there who need your unique take on education!

So, whether you're still in the classroom or already running a 1:1 tuition business, you may need a little help to move you off the fence when it comes to deciding whether or not to go all in on running just one, streamlined group tuition or coaching programme. Allow me to support you in making the right choice for you.

Chapter 2

My story

Before you dive in, I'd like to give you some context and background about what led me here. Why, after a 'successful' 10-year career teaching languages (MFL) in the UK classroom, did I decide to leave it all behind?

At 23, I gave the corporate world a bash for a while, which had some great perks. However, longing to use my languages and make a difference, I ditched the company car and dived headfirst into my language teaching career, where I spent ten turbulent years fighting with the system. Every day felt like walking a tightrope as I tried to keep up the fight to keep language-learning alive, while simultaneously trying not to get buried under the strain of what was a flawed, broken education system.

Unwilling to choose between a questionable, draining career and motherhood, the birth of my daughter saw me close the door on the classroom in 2013. Determined to give my daughter a better start in her formative years, and to bring her up with a sense of awe and humility for the world, I embarked on my quest to make language learning mainstream in the UK. I realised as I looked into my baby's innocent little squinty eyes that this was a monumental task that couldn't be tackled top-down. It had to start at the ground up, at grassroots level. With the birth of my baby, the seed of a business idea, 'BilinguaSing,' was born too.

Up until this point, I had worked with children and young

adults ranging from four to eighteen, but now, suddenly, I had a precious little baby in the world. I started a small 'Spanish through music' class with my own little girl and a group of local mums. I had no idea how it would grow and develop, but it just felt like the natural thing to do. We had so much fun and I used this group to develop what is now a unique, sensory music class with a second language at its heart. What surprised me most was the high demand!

This was when I decided to franchise the business. I had created a class that was unique and so valuable to my own community. I had done all the hard work creating music, content and a brand that was now bigger than just me and I was ready to share it with the world. When I took on my first four pilot franchisees, I was terrified; but after seeing their success, I knew it was right, and I could see the potential for further growth. Watching more and more families become inspired by language learning, with parents re-writing their stories of being terrible at languages at school, and finding a new zest for life, felt like nothing else!

Having frequent conversations with MFL teachers interested in joining our franchise network has allowed me to stay informed about the challenging situation in schools. In 2018, it struck me that I could leverage my business knowledge to support teachers from various subjects and stages who aspire to pursue their teaching dreams independently of the education system, and independently of a fixed location, too. That realisation led me to establish my online coaching business that year. Since then, I have found great joy in assisting numerous teachers in bringing their own businesses to life in the online education space.

I will never regret my teaching career. I have some wonderful memories, and I made many friends who are still important to me today. The tough times were character-building, and for much of it I am grateful. It's what led me to BilinguaSing, to my 2-Hour Tutor coaching business, and to you reading this book.

But life shouldn't be a continual endurance test. I wanted to be happier, calmer, less reactive, less frantic. I wanted to be a better mum. I just had to dare to give this dream a chance, instead of just living what had become my default.

If I could go back and talk to that young idealistic girl filling out her UCAS form, I wouldn't tell her to stop, because there would be rich life lessons to be learned through becoming a school teacher. I would just tell her to believe in herself more and to have the courage to make a change sooner when things don't feel right. We don't have to suffer, there is always another way. No matter where we are at in life, it's never too late to turn a corner (my oldest client, Jean, is 70 years old at the point of me writing this, and she is fabulous)!

I hope each page of this book brings you a sense of refreshing possibility - the possibility that your life can be less overwhelming and instead be more joyful, peaceful and fulfilling. You can still make a huge difference to others and stay true to your values, while taking time for yourself and your loved ones. It can be scary taking that leap into the unknown, but the *2-Hour Tutor TM method* is designed to support you every step of the way!

Chapter 3

The solution

1:1 tuition can feel like the obvious get-out from your teaching job, until you get really busy teaching all sorts of things to all sorts of people. Whilst this is a very nice problem to have, it always leads to very specific pain points.

Firstly – you've swapped your 60h-a-week teaching job for an intensely busy 1:1 tuition business, and you find yourself:

- Barely reducing your workload despite switching to 1:1 tuition due to the time-consuming tasks of lesson planning, admin, and marketing—leading to a quick route to burnout.
- Experiencing uncertain earnings compared to your teaching job, as income drops when clients are sick, on holiday, or when you take a break (God forbid!).
- Receiving enquiries for tuition, but having no space to accommodate them due to your limited time and capacity.
- Watching these perfect, ideal students opt to buy from someone else because you cannot serve them immediately.

If you're tired of dealing with endless planning, various subjects, and catering to clients of different levels and ages, it's time to consider a different approach. Imagine serving a group of like-minded clients who all share the same learning goals and outcomes instead.

That's precisely the model my clients and I use today, and I absolutely love it!

And here's the best part: whenever an ideal student seeks your support, you can readily offer it! No more saying, "I'm fully booked" or "I can only help you in three months."

So, how do we transition from one-on-one to a group programme? It's as simple as three essential steps:

1. Design a flexible programme structure that accommodates students joining at any time.
2. With my 2-Hour Tutor Programme Structure, you can seamlessly integrate content, live support, and a supportive community.
3. To achieve continuous growth, commit to a straightforward marketing strategy that consistently attracts new individuals who are seeking your services. Make it a weekly endeavour to bring fresh faces into your world.
4. Additionally, create a sales cycle that naturally and sustainably enrols new students every single month. It's all about establishing a system that facilitates regular enrolment and nurtures potential students until they are ready to join your programme.

And that's precisely what I assist tutors with in my online mentorship programme, The 2-Hour Tutor. Contrary to popular belief, a streamlined group programme can have an even greater impact on your students' lives than 1:1 teaching.

Embrace this approach, and you'll experience significant growth and fulfilment in your tutoring journey. Here are 7 compelling reasons why you absolutely deserve to invest in yourself and dive into this exciting tuition model:

Flexibility: Imagine having the power to set your own schedule! With a group tuition business, you'll enjoy the freedom to work when it suits you best. No more rigid timetables to hold you back!

1. More earning potential: Say goodbye to limitations on your income! Running your own business puts you in the driver's seat, giving you the potential to earn way more than traditional teaching or one-on-one tutoring ever could.
2. Time for YOU: Embrace the beauty of work-life balance! A group tuition business allows you to streamline your life and create space for all those things that regular teaching or one-on-one tutoring can't quite accommodate.
3. Pursue your passion: Are you itching to teach that one subject you're insanely passionate about? Well, starting a group tuition business lets you go all-in on your favourite topic and share your enthusiasm with eager learners.
4. Curriculum creativity: Break free from the standard cookie-cutter approach! Design your own curriculum, tailored to specific needs and interests, and leave a lasting impression as the go-to expert in your field.
5. Reach your ideal students: With a group tuition business, you can reach a wider pool of students who are just perfect for your teaching style. Impacting more learners at once? Now, that's a game-changer!

6. Personal growth galore: Running your own business means learning valuable new life skills that will serve you both personally and professionally. It's a win-win!

While traditional classroom teaching works for many, running a streamlined group tuition business offers an even greater opportunity for you to invest in yourself, grow personally and professionally, and have more time and money . . . all while making a meaningful impact on the lives of your students.

So, buckle up, grab your journal, and let's get started on this transformative journey. Your health, happiness and finances will thank you for it!

Chapter 4

'Unschool' your mind

Let's dive into how to mentally prepare for this transformative journey. This is more than just a guide book; you are holding the keys to your next level self - this is exciting stuff; but we have to clear the decks first. We'll need to address long-held habits, beliefs, and thoughts that may be holding you back. We need to 'unlearn' what we currently believe about what is possible for ourselves.

Firstly, let's talk about mindset. As teachers, we often face difficult times, but I want you to embrace your Professional Pride. You have credibility that most tutors don't possess. Your status as a school teacher, your degree, postgraduate qualifications, and experience must not be undervalued.

I understand that, as teachers, we've learned to accept being undervalued for a long time, but together, we can work on that as we move forward.

I want you to step into your industry confidently, not playing small. You can command higher prices, and I don't want you to compare yourself to others. We'll work on building a strong, ethical tutoring business that won't tire you out with endless one-to-one tuition.

All I ask is that you approach this change with an open mind and heart. Acknowledge that we need to change and be prepared for challenges and difficult conversations with loved ones, friends, and colleagues. Carving out dedicated time for this over the coming weeks and months will be essential.

Self-belief

Self-belief is crucial, but it doesn't always come first. Many of us want to feel confident before taking a leap into something new, but we must embrace fear and discomfort as part of the process. Say "thanks" to fear, acknowledge it, but don't let it hold you back. Remember, if your dreams don't scare you, they might not be big enough!

Dealing with doubt and other people's questions

Prepare for sceptical people asking questions like, "Why are you doing this?" Have an off-the-shelf response ready. Emphasise that the world is changing, and online opportunities are abundant. Remind yourself that following the crowd doesn't always lead to true security, and that you have to be brave if you want your life to change.

Embrace the uncertainty of the future. It's full of potential.

Addressing guilt

Feelings of guilt may arise during this process, but it's normal. Don't let guilt deter you. Instead, recognise the dedication and time you've invested in your current career, and putting others

first. Focus on the positive impact you've made and the opportunity it has given you to grow in a new direction.

Journalling and reflection

Consider keeping a journal to process your feelings, thoughts, and experiences throughout this transformation. Take five or ten minutes each day to reflect on your journey, during the quietest part of the day (I am a night owl - so I prefer to do this when my husband and three kids are sleeping)! This will help you maintain the right mindset and keep your goals clear.

As an experienced teacher, you already have all the transferable skills you need to make this journey achievable. Even if you have only known the inside of a classroom throughout your educational and working life, you have so many valuable skills that you can now "pack for the journey," having done perhaps the most difficult job there is. Embrace the fear and uncertainty, challenge old beliefs, and remember that the world is changing; it's absolutely right (and necessary!) that we should change with it.

Embrace this period of transformation, and believe in yourself and your ability to succeed in building your new future. You are a teacher, which makes you a remarkable human. I believe in you!

Take stock

A great coaching tool for 'clearing the decks' is the Wheel of Life.

This is an example of a life wheel, the Wheel of Life. Hopefully, you've got a nice shiny new journal on its way now, ready for you to do a few exercises.

This is all about measuring and assessing where you are now. I'd really like you to do this before you even start thinking about what kind of group programme you'd like to run.

Draw a circle and divide it into eight segments, labelling each one: emotional wellbeing, work/career, finances, health and fitness, family relationships, personal growth, and fun/leisure (if you're reading a hard copy of this book then feel free to fill out the wheel diagram above).

These core areas of our life should be relatively in balance for us to feel happy and have the freedom we want. Shade in each segment to the level you think reflects where you currently are. This can be quite telling - confronting, even.

My own wheel had low scores in various areas: emotional wellbeing and fun/leisure were at about a three. Work/career was around a six or five, finances at about a three, health and fitness maybe a four or five, family relationships needed improvement as I wasn't prioritising them enough.

Personal growth also felt stunted, hitting a ceiling early on in my teaching career. Fun/leisure wasn't great either. So, my wheel had a few sixes, maybe a seven, but lots of threes and even twos.

Be honest with yourself about where you are now. If you're considering going back to teaching or transitioning to a new teaching job, imagine how you'd feel in that scenario. We'll talk more about this later, and it'll serve as a record of your progress as you implement what you learn in this book.

Chapter 5

The Happy and Free Success Mindset

I want to share with you the principles of a happy and free success mindset that will propel you towards achieving your best and experiencing success as you build your 2-Hour Tuition business.

Rule 1: Police your thoughts

It all starts with being mindful of our thoughts. Often, we unconsciously tell ourselves limiting beliefs like "I can't" or "I'm not good enough." Just think about yourself as one of your students - you wouldn't repeatedly tell a pupil that they were not capable or good enough, would you? The key is to catch ourselves in these moments and reframe those negative thoughts into positive ones. Instead of saying, "I can't do this," try affirming, "I am learning how to X, Y, Z." By doing this, we shift our mindset to one that embraces growth and possibilities.

Rule 2: Be compassionate towards yourself

As you embark on this journey, be kind to yourself. Mistakes and setbacks are part of the learning process. If you don't get something right the first time, remember that you're a work inprogress (just like your own students will be). Embrace the fact that you are constantly learning and evolving. Practice self-love and patience; it's okay to take your time to master new skills and concepts. If we don't, we stagnate!

Rule 3: Be resilient and robust

Life is full of challenges, and the path to success is rarely smooth. But that's where our resilience comes into play. Embrace the hurdles and setbacks as opportunities for growth. Don't be discouraged by obstacles; instead, see them as stepping stones to a stronger, more accomplished version of yourself. Stay robust in your determination and know that you can overcome any obstacle that comes your way. You're a teacher - which makes you superhuman!

Rule 4: Burn your bridges

Decide that there is no plan B. You have made a commitment to yourself and your goals, and you will see it through. It's normal to face moments of doubt and difficulty, but remember that giving up is not an option. You're not going back; you're only moving forward towards greater things. Keep your eyes on the prize, and the journey will be all the more rewarding.

Rule 5: Practice patience

Rome wasn't built in a day, and nor was my business, or any other for that matter. Success takes time, effort, and dedication. Be patient with the process and trust that

progress is happening, even if it's not always visible. Remember, it is not a race; it's a journey of growth and self-discovery. Utilise all the tools and resources at your disposal, and celebrate every small victory along the way.

Rule 6: Imperfect is great!

Perfectionism can be paralysing. Waiting for the perfect moment or the perfect idea can prevent us from taking action. Embrace imperfection and understand that it's okay to start with something that may not be flawless. All the best companies start with a Minimal Viable Product (a bog-standard prototype of their idea) and they just get it out there. What matters is that you start and progress forward. Imperfect is great because it means you're doing, and doing is how you learn, improve, and ultimately succeed.

By adopting this 'happy and free' success mindset, you'll transform the way you approach challenges, setbacks, and opportunities. Embrace your journey with patience, resilience, and self-compassion.

Remember, there's no plan B; you're *all in*. Believe in yourself, take that imperfect step forward, and watch yourself grow and achieve greatness in the coming weeks, months and beyond!

The power of endurance in pursuing success

I want to share a powerful message that resonates deeply with anyone on the journey towards success. Often, we find ourselves waiting for the perfect moment, the ideal

circumstances, or the right skills to get started. But, in reality, success isn't about having it all; it's about the endurance to keep going, no matter the obstacles or imperfections.

The endurance mindset: As I recorded my course videos for the 2-Hour Tutor Programme, there would be occasional chaos in the background - doors closing, kids shouting, and the messiness of real life. Despite these distractions, I didn't (and still won't) wait for the perfect conditions to share important messages with my clients. Perfectionism is overrated, and realness is what connects us. People relate to authenticity, and that's what I strive to bring to my videos.

> "I was considering Ellie's course for some time, and one day she published a video where she was sitting in her car with her kids' mess and car seats visible, wearing no makeup and laughing at herself for being imperfect. That was the moment I decided she was the coach for me!"
>
> Claire Davidson, English tutor

Talent vs. Endurance: Success isn't about being the smartest or most talented person in the room. As educators, you already possess incredible skills and expertise. What sets successful individuals apart is their unwavering endurance. They keep going, pushing forward, and refusing to give up. It's about staying committed to your goals and not getting discouraged by challenges or setbacks.

Embrace the lows: Throughout your journey, there will be moments of excitement and inspiration. But there will also be lows when you feel frustrated, tired, or stuck. Embrace these moments; they are part of the process. Recognise that it's normal to face hurdles and difficulties.

The key is to keep going despite these lows, maintaining your focus on the finish line.

The power of determination: Success is not about how many talents or advantages you possess. It's about the determination to endure, to persevere, and to keep moving forward, even when things get tough. Don't let comparisons with others deter you. The only comparison that matters is the one you make with your past self. Celebrate your progress and focus on your journey.

Remember, you have what it takes to succeed. You are uniquely talented, and your commitment to endurance will propel you forward. Embrace your authenticity, and don't wait for perfection to get started. Keep pushing forward, and you will achieve the success you desire. Keep going, keep growing, and keep embracing the journey to success.

> "If you want to take the island, then burn your boats. With absolute commitment comes the insights that create real victory."
>
> Tony Robbins

Being 'in it' 100% is far easier than giving it just 95%. Tell yourself there is no way back. If there is a way back, the ego will have room to convince you to stay as you are. Remember – we are programmed not to change. When our ancestors detected change, it was life-threatening because the sabre-toothed tiger was on the prowl.

Chapter 6
Time to clear the decks

In this section, we'll delve into the topic of decluttering and creating space for positive transformations in our lives.

To start, we need to clear out the things we no longer wish to keep in our lives, making way for new opportunities. Take some time to reflect on what you no longer want to accept. You can jot down your thoughts in a journal for this purpose.

We'll start with decluttering and then, once we have created the necessary space, we can focus on what we can bring into our lives to help us dedicate time and energy to our transformation.

Smartphone or dim-phone?

Let's begin by addressing social media habits. Social media can be a significant time sink, while also causing feelings of inadequacy when comparing ourselves to others. So, I recommend going through your social media accounts and unfollowing people and pages that don't add value to your life. Consider keeping only a few inspiring individuals in your feed who promote personal growth and development.

You can even take it a step further by deleting unnecessary apps from your phone or limiting the time spent on them. By doing so, you can gain back valuable time to invest in the journey ahead.

Time-sucking habits

Next, let's tackle other time-sucking habits. Identify activities that don't contribute positively to your life, like mindless scrolling, binge-watching, or reading excessive news. Commit to refraining from these habits for at least 12 weeks. This will save you time and help you maintain focus on your personal growth journey.

Emotional spending

Emotional spending is another area we should address. Think about the times you spend money to feel better, like impulse purchases or indulging in comfort food. Challenge yourself to cut back on such spending and focus on investing in your personal growth instead.

Friendships

Remember, personal growth might lead to changes in your friendships, and that's okay. Forgive those who may not understand your journey. There can be various reasons why some people may not seem happy or enthusiastic when you share news about your new project. People's reactions and emotions are complex, and their responses may not always align with your expectations. Here are some possible reasons why they might not appear as excited as you'd hope:

> *Jealousy or envy*: Sometimes, people can feel envious or jealous when they hear about friends' accomplishments or

new projects. This could be due to their own insecurities or a sense of competition. Instead of being genuinely happy for you, they may feel a tinge of resentment.

Fear of change: People can be apprehensive about change, especially if they perceive your new project as something that might alter your relationship with them or your current dynamic. They may worry about how this change could impact your friendship or whether they'll be left behind as you move on.

Past experiences: Past experiences can shape how people respond to new information. If they've had negative experiences with trying to quit teaching or starting a tuition business, they might be projecting their fears and sense of failure onto you.

Consider the people you interact with regularly. Are there some friends or colleagues who bring you down or discourage your aspirations? It's okay to spend less time with such people or adjust how much you choose to share with them. Surround yourself with those who support and encourage your growth instead.

Physical decluttering

Maybe there's an ornament in your house that someone bought you for Christmas years ago, or for your wedding, that you just find hideous. But you feel so guilty at the thought of getting rid of it.

I received a lovely but creepy meerkat carving from one of my aunties as a wedding gift (bless her). While I held onto it for quite some time, I eventually came to realise that I didn't actually like it. Every time I saw it, I felt guilty because I knew I wanted to part with it. Eventually, I decided to donate it to a charity. The sense of relief was palpable; I swear I could almost feel the extra space free up in my mind and body as well as the cupboard shelf it occupied!

You know, it's essential to be mindful of the things that don't bring us joy. Have you heard of Marie Kondo, the famous Japanese declutterer? She believes that if an object doesn't serve a purpose for you or bring you joy when you look at it, hold it, or wear it, then it's time to let it go.

I'm not suggesting a complete decluttering of your entire house right now. Instead, focus on adopting a decluttering mindset. Set aside a specific area to work on your new 2-Hour Tutor project, transforming it into a beautiful, calming, and organised space.

Declutter this one space for now, providing yourself with a spacious environment that won't weigh you down or remind you of unfinished projects, unworn clothes, non-functional gifts, broken items, or things you simply don't like.

Make room for nice notepads and shiny new pens. Allow space in your wardrobe for the beautiful things you'll eventually be able to buy for yourself. When you've achieved your goals and have your programme out there, you'll be able to fill those gaps with beautiful things that bring you joy.

Repeat to yourself: *"Things that no longer serve me are needed elsewhere. My trash is someone else's treasure."*

Charities frequently collect furniture, and you can donate

clothes in good condition to them. If something has a minor issue, consider getting it repaired or explore options like Thrift: an online second-hand platform that enables you to sell your clothes and donate a portion of the proceeds to charity.

Think about decluttering one thing each week—maybe your wardrobe next week, or your office space. This makes room for new things, a new life, and items that genuinely bring you joy. You don't need loads of stuff, just a few things that truly make you happy. It's time to 'call in' the future you want to create, by setting your intentions for it right now.

Chapter 7

Habits for success

Reprogramming our beliefs

Now, let's consider beliefs that don't serve you. Take a moment to identify the negative thoughts you often tell yourself, such as 'I'm not clever enough,' 'I hate technology' or 'no-one in my family has ever had a successful business.'

Write down these beliefs, then symbolically let go of them. Tear the paper or draw a big cross through them and replace each with a positive, empowering belief. For example, change 'I'm not clever enough' to 'I am a fast learner and can grasp new concepts quickly.'

Remember the 'Happy and Free Teacher mindset' rules? It's essential to police your thoughts, as they shape your beliefs. By actively monitoring and challenging these negative beliefs, you can foster positive change and cultivate beliefs that serve you better.

Set your Daily Standards

Okay, now the exciting part begins. We are going to set your Daily Standards.

What are the things you want to add to your life? What daily standards will you uphold for yourself? We've already discussed what you're letting go of, so now let's focus on what you want to build into your daily routine to create a supportive structure for a new life.

Move your body

Let's start by committing to moving your body every day. It doesn't matter if you're into exercise or if your schedule makes it challenging. Find a way to move daily. It could be a walk during lunchtime, waking up a bit earlier for an exercise routine, or even a 10-minute yoga session before bed.

Write down an activity that you can do without any excuses. Aim for at least 10 minutes, but 20 minutes would be great, and if you can manage 30 minutes, even better. Remember, it's not necessary to go beyond 30 minutes.

Moving your body not only keeps you fit and healthy but also supports a strong mindset during this period of change. It's essential to have a healthy body and mind to succeed. Successful people move their bodies every day. So, decide what activity you want to do and commit to it. For me, yoga is my way to wind down after a long day. Once the kids are asleep, you can find me on my mat in the kitchen, following a YouTube video of Yoga with Adriene. It has been truly life-changing for me. That's just one recommendation, but you can choose any activity that suits you. So, get moving and enjoy the benefits of a clearer, more focused mind straight away!

Systemise and automate

As a teacher (or former teacher), I'm sure you have successfully relied on certain systems and processes to help you get through the day and get things done. A mark scheme, for example, is one such system. As teachers, we tend to be more creatively inclined and not particularly fond of systems. However, I've come to appreciate the power of systemization and automation in my business. By implementing processes for almost everything, I've gained the freedom, time, and financial stability I always wanted for my family. It has also allowed me to give back in ways I never imagined possible.

When I started my teaching career in 2003, we didn't have the technological resources we have today. Overhead projectors and tatty textbooks were the norm, and even the laptops were limited. However, around 2007, I was granted the first whiteboard in the MFL department, and it completely changed my perspective. I began systemising and organising resources digitally, which proved to be immensely helpful later when I moved to a different school.

In the world of online business, technology offers endless opportunities to enhance and streamline processes. With various low-cost or free software tools, almost everything can be organised, systemised, and automated. Embracing technology is crucial in this new era, and it won't replace people but empower those who use it effectively.

Now, let's talk about running a successful online group tuition business. I'll teach you all the marketing know-how you need, but we can't ignore the role of essential tools like email service providers, design software, and of course, Zoom.

These tools can be used simply and freely or more sophisticatedly if you love tech. However, I don't want the tech to hinder you from launching your tuition business; it's not a prerequisite. What matters most is getting out there, engaging with your ideal customers, and making money.

Teaching is a noble profession, but unfortunately, many teachers face challenges due to low pay and lack of respect. It's time for a change, and I've learned this firsthand after leaving the teaching profession. Now, I help teachers create a brighter future, offering potential, financial abundance, and freedom. With a solid method and the right mindset, you can replace your teacher salary and lead a fulfilling life.

So, stay with me on this journey, and I'll provide you with the necessary steps and mindset training to become a happy and successful online tutor. Let's begin this exciting chapter together!

Let's start with the home

Now let's focus on creating systems and automation to make our home life easier. Consider how to systemise or automate tasks every week. For instance, instead of spending time at the supermarket, opt for home delivery with an automated shopping list. Save your regular items in an app and make small tweaks as needed.

During lockdown, I started using a milk delivery service, which has been fantastic. They deliver milk, bread, and eggs, ensuring we never run out of essentials while being environmentally friendly. Look for a local dairy that offers similar services.

To promote healthy eating without going out, consider getting a veggie box delivered. It's a convenient way to ensure you have nutritious food at hand. Oddbox is cheap and cheerful, if budget is a concern.

Managing finances can be streamlined with a spreadsheet. You can find helpful recommendations and financial spreadsheets on YouTube or Etsy, like Mama FurFur's channel. Even better, consider switching to a bank like Monzo which automatically tracks expenditure which you can categorise with a simple click. Let tech do the heavy lifting wherever you can!

Identify stress triggers, such as end-of-month financial worries, and find ways to automate payments or budgeting to ease the burden.

Investing in a cleaner early on in my business has turned out to be a wise decision. It has allowed me to dedicate more time to my family and growing my business. As a result, I now have an extra 6 hours per week that I can utilise to find new clients and provide excellent service to my existing ones. This increased focus on the core aspects of my business has significantly boosted my earnings, surpassing the amount I spend on cleaning services.

Additionally, hiring a cleaner has had a positive impact on someone else's life, as they get the opportunity to earn their own income through the services they provide. It's truly a win-win situation for both of us.

Initially, I started with just 2 hours of help every fortnight. However, with three kids and three furry animals in the house,

things deteriorated quickly between cleans. Gradually, I upgraded to a twice-weekly cleaning service, which has made a huge difference in maintaining a tidy and clean environment and reducing my mental and physical load. I've seen how having even a fortnightly cleaner has been a game-changer for my teacher friends as well. It shifts your mindset about having to constantly keep the house tidy and clean. Knowing that someone will come and sort it out at some point helps you relax and focus on other priorities.

In the past, I used to feel embarrassed about admitting that I had a cleaner, fearing it might make me seem 'spoiled' or 'entitled.' However, I've come to realise that these thoughts were just my inner critic speaking. It's perfectly acceptable to seek help with household chores, especially if it allows me to concentrate on my family and self-care, and help others through my coaching programme. Not only does it benefit my business, but it also makes me a more relaxed and attentive mum - which is at the top of my values list. Now, my kids get the best version of me, as I can spend quality time with them instead of constantly stressing about cleaning and tidying up.

Are there any tasks, such as cleaning or others, that you could systemise and automate to simplify your life and free up time to focus on your new venture? Brainstorm some now and commit to three things. Then make them happen!

Connect with like-minded people

We have examined how certain people can drain our energy and hinder our progress. Now, it's essential to surround yourself with like-minded individuals who share your aspirations.

Consider the friends and acquaintances you have. Are there any individuals among them who you admire? Those who have pursued their dreams and set up businesses, regardless of whether they were teachers like you or not. Reach out to them, connect, and ask if they'd be interested in meeting for a coffee. Share with them your new venture.

Look for opportunities to mix with people who can uplift and guide you towards becoming the person you aspire to be - someone who is a step ahead or has already achieved what you desire. Take some time to think about the right connections that can lead you to your new self. Connect with them, learn from them, and let them lift you up.

Schedule and dedicate

Let's prioritise the things that matter to you by creating a schedule. Personally, I find using my phone's calendar (iCal) helpful. I schedule time to dedicate to my priorities so that I can manage my time effectively. My daily routine includes some form of exercise in the morning, four days a week, and a few evenings dedicated to yoga, though it can vary depending on how I feel. If I miss something, I make sure to reschedule it later in the week.

For those who embark on my course (The 2-Hour Tutor), now that they've eliminated time-wasting habits, they allocate a specific time slot each day to work through the programme consistently. It could be something as simple as dedicating half an hour for journaling and watching the next video in my programme. Determine what you'll do, and when, ahead of time. This will make it easier to fit what's important into your schedule now that you've cleared away unnecessary time-consumers.

Learning and developing

As a teacher seeking a life of meaning and freedom, it's essential to invest in daily learning and development. Congratulations for taking the first step with this book, where I will teach you all about my 2-Hour Tutor method. Make sure to schedule and dedicate time to learning and implementing the steps I lay out in this book, and you'll see yourself progress quickly.

What you concentrate on, you attract more of. If you want this to be your future, give it your all. Your positivity and focus will lead to better and quicker results.

Chapter 8

Letting go compassionately

Thank You Teaching

This one can really be quite cathartic. There will be times when you'll reminisce over the good things about teaching, and feel pangs of nostalgia. It's important that we honour our teaching days, and carry forward all the good that came from it.

There are so many transferable skills linked with teaching that are relevant to business management – communication, time-keeping, patience, resilience, resourcefulness, being able to live well outside of your comfort zone, and being self-sufficient (there is no such thing as Personal Assistant when you're a teacher)!

Despite leaving the classroom in 2013 to start my own kids language class business, BilinguaSing, I find myself referring back to my teacher training, regularly.

But when I was working as a teacher, my time was so stretched that I hardly had the time to realise I was using this skillset.

Today, my sister Mel and I, both former teachers, continue to run and grow this business together. It's a real privilege that we've been able to franchise our business model and help other language teachers kickstart their own businesses. The best part is, we didn't need any fancy qualifications or extra training – just our teacher skillset, a willingness to invest in great coaches and mentors, and a passion for continuous learning and growth.

With your teaching skills on your side, you can create a life and business that gives you the freedom to level up your professional game and secure a brighter future. Trust me, there is a whole new world out there waiting for you! Exciting opportunities are ahead.

Conscious uncoupling

This exercise focuses on gratitude and the positive aspects of being a teacher. We want to reflect on what teaching has brought us and what we are grateful for, leaving behind any negative aspects.

You can use prompts to help you with this exercise. Consider using a pen and paper, a mind map, bullet points, or starting a gratitude journal. One suggestion is to write a letter breaking up with teaching, expressing thanks for the positive experiences and acknowledging what you'll miss.

Reflect on the highs and the gifts teaching has given you. Acknowledge moments of joy, the friendships formed, and the development of resilience and self-awareness. Confidence may have been affected in different ways, and that's okay—explore how teaching has shaped your self-esteem.

Understand that even mistakes and challenging experiences have brought wisdom, making you who you are today. Embrace the learnings and carry them forward as you part ways with teaching in a positive way.

Feel free to share your reflections with someone if you'd like, or keep them private. Maybe buddy up with a friend so you can both keep yourselves accountable. The goal is to be thankful for the positive impact teaching has had on your life so that you can move forward without hanging on to bitterness and resentment. By 'clearing the decks' in this way we can make headspace for what we really want.

For example, do you want to work two days a week and bring home more money than you did (or do) working five-day weeks as a teacher? Declare it!

Do you finally want to reclaim your time for your family, have the money for nice, long holidays and a quality of life that you never imagined?

Don't hold back. There are plenty of other tutors out there making a huge impact and being financially rewarded for it. Why not you? It's your time to dream big.

Well done, we have done some significant work in clearing the decks in this chapter. Now we are ready to move forward with planning your exit strategy, and creating the ideal 2-Hour Tutor programme for you. Buckle up - this is going to be a fun ride!

Personality profiling - a powerful tool for change

One bonus we are delighted to be able to offer our members is personality profiling; a truly rich and insightful process that will help you gain a deeper understanding of yourself and your personality type.

This, combined with your Values Hierarchy and your Mission Statement give you the 'three pillars' that will underpin every decision you make going forward.

We have our very own Mindset Coach, Terry Hill (also known as Dad!), who is not only a best-selling author with his book, The Inspiration Code, but also boasts extensive experience in personality profiling. It's only natural that I'm utilising this incredible expertise to benefit my clients.

A personality profiling session with a qualified coach can help you to:

- Know your strengths and weaknesses: discover your natural abilities and areas for improvement, boosting your confidence and effectiveness as a tutor.
- Discover your unique tutoring approach: Learn how you solve problems, communicate, and work effectively online, enabling you to adapt your teaching style to match your unique personality, enhancing the learning experience for your students.
- Improve communication: Understand your preferred communication style, fostering better connections with like-minded students and their parents, leading to smoother relationships.
- Find the right tutoring niche: Identify your passions and strengths to guide you in selecting the best area to specialise in, allowing you to shine as a tutor.

Our 2-Hour Tutor personality profiling empowers you to be a successful and fulfilled tutor, unlocking your tutoring potential, and making an even more positive impact on your students' lives.

Chapter 9

Feel the fear

In this section, we're discussing fear once again, which I know might be a recurring theme. Fear never truly disappears; it resurfaces repeatedly, especially when we seek growth in our lives or businesses.

Whenever we level up, there's a new layer of fear to confront, and that's perfectly normal. Instead of being afraid of fear, let's make peace with it. Fear is often just False Evidence Appearing Real – it's a construct of our minds.

In the past, fear served a purpose, protecting us from immediate threats like sabre-toothed tigers. But today, such life-threatening situations are rare. So, we should recognise fear as a part of our natural defence mechanism and acknowledge its presence.

"If this change is genuinely for the better, why am I so scared?" you might wonder. It's because fear often accompanies growth; it's an inevitable part of the process. Think back to your initial fear of walking into a classroom. It only faded as you repeatedly faced it, gradually transforming (if you were ever fortunate enough!) into a sense of sweet anticipation. The less encouraging part is that fear will persist until you take that leap, as evolution and our upbringing have wired us to err on the side of caution. After all, how often do mothers tell their children, "Don't forget to take some risks today, darling!"

So, have you been allowing FEAR to hold you back? Maybe it's kept you in your job for too long, or you're not sure how to let go of those less-than-ideal tutoring clients in order to go all in on one programme for one kind of student.

Fear of change, especially in our work-life, is completely normal. Money fears are something we all face. I once asked my own business coach, "Does the fear ever completely disappear?" Her response was straightforward: "No."

I had believed that reaching a specific income level or achieving a particular milestone would somehow make the fear vanish. However, that's not the case. (At least, I haven't discovered it yet.)
So here are some truths about fear that may give you a fresh perspective:

- Playing the game of business is scary - but staying in a miserable job is too.

- You'll be out of your comfort zone a lot - but then you probably already are.

- Asking for money is scary - but facing a future of being broke is even more so.

- Setting boundaries is scary - but letting others direct your life forever is terrifying.

- Saying 'no' is scary - but continually saying 'yes' to a situation we don't even want is petrifying!

See the pattern?

As humans our greatest challenge is fear, but it doesn't have to stop you from chasing your dreams. You just need to ensure that your desire to go after your dreams is stronger than your fear (even if it's just a little bit).

Does your DESIRE to help more students outweigh your fear?

Does your longing for financial abundance and more free time overshadow your fear?

Is the dream of a new home for your family, or a round-the-world trip worthy enough of your attention, or will the fear win out?

You don't have to be superhero-brave. Just focus on gradually replacing fear with your desires by giving your dreams a bit more of your time and attention.

As the old Hindi saying goes,

'Where focus goes, energy flows.'

And where energy flows, whatever you're focusing on grows. In other words, your life will head in the direction of what you focus on. That's why you need to focus on where you want to go, not on what you fear.

Instead of focusing on *what isn't yet* - focus on *what could be*. Then it will start showing up for you.

Just try it!

> Bookmark this section or remember where to find it, so you can revisit it whenever fear arises. Remember, change is scary for all of us, but it's essential to confront it. The alternative of staying in our comfort zones is even scarier – the regret of missed opportunities a decade later is truly terrifying.

If you want to grow as a person, accept fear's presence and embrace it. Consider fear as a doorway that stands between you and your future, your new self. If you allow fear to control you, you'll remain stagnant, never evolving.

Let's not allow fear to block our path to personal growth. Instead, try two exercises whenever fear takes hold of you:

> Imagine your life in two years, with and without making the change you desire. Feel how each scenario affects you emotionally. Tear up the vision you don't want and keep the one you desire somewhere visible to remind you of your goals.

> Find a quiet space, close your eyes, and visualise the outcome of taking action versus not taking action. Notice which scenario brings relief, happiness, joy, and empowerment.

Fear may not vanish, but by deciding how we respond to it, we can take control. Keep this section for future reference and practise these exercises whenever fear overwhelms you.

Chapter 10

Deciding on your ideal programme

Step 1 - Uncover your values

Now, let's move on to discovering your values, the solid foundation for everything else. We've got an exercise that will help you dig deep and uncover what truly matters to you.

Values are a key indicator of our level of happiness. In simple terms:

- Alignment (harmony) = Happiness
- Misalignment = Stress

So, what does it mean to start making aligned choices?

It means saying no to things that don't feel right, and saying yes to what does. It's time to find out what really lights you up!

Once you've got a good handle on your values, it's time to explore your 'mission' or what you want to achieve in life. This step is crucial because it helps us align our path with what we truly believe in.

Once you've nailed down your values and mission, it's time to check out some tuition ideas and options. What kind of programs can you explore that match up with your values and purpose? We'll be looking at different courses and figuring out which ones are the best fit for you.

And finally, we'll put together a solid action plan to make things happen. Armed with your values, mission, and options, we'll set up actionable steps that will lead you towards your dream future.

By the end of this chapter, you'll have a clear idea of your next moves, free from any outside pressures or what others might think. We'll be focusing on what really matters to you and creating a path that aligns with your deepest dreams and aspirations.

You may have jumped into teaching with all your values aligned, thinking that it would fulfil you. For me, discovering that this would never be the case was painful. I felt cheated, let down and powerless to change the failing education system. I realised I couldn't fix it alone, and that for now I would have to focus on filling my own cup first. Getting myself sorted would enable me to contribute to something bigger than myself later down the line. Staying and martyring myself to this broken system would be hypocritical, as so much of it went against everything I believe education should be (and still does)!

Let's talk about values now because that's so key here. Martin Luther King said, "If a man hasn't found something that he will die for, then he isn't fit to live." Living without values can leave us questioning our purpose in life and avoiding that question by distracting ourselves with other things.

Tony Robbins emphasises that there is no success except in keeping with your values. Values are those things that individuals will invest time and energy in, to either achieve or avoid. Most people spend time and money on distractions rather than doing the deep, inner work required to explore what their true values are.

Stress and burnout often come from living out of alignment with our values. But when you're doing something in line with your values, you'll never feel burnt out. Clarity on our values is essential for success, which is personally defined and shouldn't be dictated by others (or some antiquated system that doesn't take into account our individuality or need for self-care).

Gandhi said, *"Happiness is when what you think, what you say, and what you do are in harmony."* That's the feeling we should have when we work in alignment with our values, completely absorbed and motivated.

To discover your values, think about when you were most motivated and fulfilled in your career. What feelings were present? What was important to you? Boil these down to five or six key words that describe what you stand for in your life and work.

Now, I want you to imagine a celebration ceremony in ten years, where you have achieved everything you wanted. You're presented with a beautiful necklace with five charms, or maybe a watch; engraved with five words describing something important to you. Take your time with this exercise and enjoy the process.

Making choices in alignment with yourself is key to feeling good and creating the life you want. Make a habit of checking in with yourself and asking: 'Does this feel good to *me*?' Choosing to let go of something misaligned creates space to invite in something worth saying YES to!

So, what are you choosing to say NO to today? And, what do you choose to say YES to?

Let's do this!

Take the values exercise a step further and create an artistic word cloud (quickly and for free): **https://monkeylearn.com/word-cloud/**

Check out mine here:

integrity
financialfreedom
family love joy
mentorship
autonomy
personalgrowth

Print it, frame it, stick in on your fridge, and set it as your phone wallpaper or desktop background so you can familiarise yourself with your values, and get to know yourself on a deeper level.

Step 2: Find your 'zone of genius'

Gay Hendricks' Zone of Genius theory is a concept that emphasises the importance of identifying and leveraging one's unique strengths and innate abilities to achieve personal fulfilment and success. According to Hendricks, there are four zones in which we tend to operate:

> **Zone of Incompetence**: This zone comprises activities or tasks in which we have little to no skill or expertise, and we struggle to perform them effectively.
>
> **Zone of Competence**: In this zone, we possess the necessary skills to perform tasks adequately, but we lack a true passion or enthusiasm for these activities.
>
> **Zone of Excellence**: Here, we excel at tasks and activities and receive recognition and praise for our competence. However, even though we may be successful in these areas, they don't make us feel fulfilled.
>
> **Zone of Genius**: The Zone of Genius is the sweet spot where we use our natural talents and passions to perform activities that bring us pure joy and satisfaction. It is the space where we can make a unique and valuable contribution to the world.

Hendricks suggests that by identifying and focusing on our

Zone of Genius, we can experience increased productivity, creativity, and fulfilment in our personal and professional lives. By devoting more time to tutoring within this zone, we can find greater purpose and make a significant impact on both our own lives and the lives of our students.

With this in mind, let's dive into finding your perfect role in the online tutoring space! First up, we want to shine a light on your skills, interests, and values to match you with the right idea.

So, think back to a time when you achieved something significant. What was the challenge? What skills did you show off, and how did you overcome any obstacles? Jot down how you achieved it, and how others saw your accomplishment.

Next, let's talk about what makes you happy and fulfilled. Imagine you've got an extra day in the week to do whatever you like just for fun. List down all those activities that bring you joy.

Now, onto your values—what truly matters to you. Take a moment to reflect on your core values and see how they align with your skills and interests. You can visualise this magic happening or draw it out in your own Venn diagram.

As we piece together your skills, interests, and values, we'll find some 'hotspots' where they intersect. That's where you'll discover your 'zone of genius' idea—the niche that fulfils you on all levels.

Keep in mind that your dream programme should align with your values and let you shine with your strengths and interests. Avoid thinking about what you 'should' do because it's probably going to be more lucrative / popular / undersaturated etc. This is the kind of 'old thinking' we want to move away from!

If this sounds tricky, just think about which aspects of teaching have brought you the most joy and felt natural to you. This will lead to the perfect tuition idea for you; one that feels easy, allows you to stand out from a sea of generalists and become a true expert.

Step 3: Decide on your way forward

Let's dive into the exciting part of the chapter, where we get to narrow down all those fantastic ideas we've unearthed through all this soul searching.

Remember those beautiful gems - your values, interests, skills, and life purpose? They are the building blocks of finding the perfect idea for your   online course!

Don't worry if you've got a tonne of ideas or just one. Embrace it all! We're here to make the process fun and straightforward. We'll create a simple yet effective table where you can jot down your ideas and score them based on your values and skills. Forget about the nitty-gritty details like delivery and marketing right now; we'll tackle those later.

The main focus is on what truly ignites your passion, what you're excited about teaching or creating, and, of course, how much joy it brings you. When you score your ideas, you'll have a clear picture of which one resonates most with you.

But wait, let's add a sprinkle of magic to the process! Close your eyes and visualise yourself actually doing the top two ideas. Feel the excitement, the energy, and the fulfilment. Score each idea based on how it makes you feel in your heart.

Now comes the moment of empowerment - commit to your chosen idea! And remember, this isn't a lifelong vow; it's simply the next step in your journey. You can always explore other paths and ventures in the future.

Now, I won't sugarcoat it. Doubts might creep in, whispering that you can't do it or that you're not good enough. But here's the secret - acknowledge those doubts, thank them for their input, and then move forward anyway. Replace them with a vivid mental image of you absolutely rocking it, making a difference, and feeling completely in your element.

You've got the power within you - you can do this! I'd love to hear about your chosen idea - feel free to email me with your progress.

Embrace the process, enjoy the journey, and keep that smile shining brightly! I'll be right here, cheering you on, as you step into the next section of this chapter with a newfound sense of purpose!

Step 4: Get your mission on!

We've finally reached the part where we create our mission. This mission will play a crucial role in propelling you forward and guiding your creations. By now, you should have an idea of your direction and target audience, and you probably have a basic idea about identifying your audience. Let's now focus on your idea and how it can bring positive change to the world and help people. Consider what you stand for and what you stand against. For example, as a languages teacher, I stand for language accessibility and inclusivity while opposing marginalisation in the curriculum.

To set yourself apart from others doing something similar, think about your ideal client and what you want them to know. For instance, I want parents to understand that language skills are essential for their children's future. Identify their struggles and misconceptions and think about how you can provide a solution.

Moreover, consider the deeper aspects of your mission. Is there a cause you're passionate about supporting or a revolution you want to start? Reflect on the ten most important lessons you've learned in life that led you here. Consider the recurring issues in your field, what you daydream about doing, and what you want to be remembered for at the end of your life. Imagine if you couldn't fail, what would you do?

Now, let's work on crafting your mission statement. You can use this template:

"My mission is to help [target audience] achieve [main desire] through [your process]. I want them to know [important message] and [another important message]. I stand against [opposing force], but I'm here to [your purpose]."

This mission statement will be the core of your marketing and everything you do.

Take your time to refine it, and remember that it can evolve as your business grows. Your mission statement should embody your passion and values, helping you stay focused on making a positive impact on your target audience. It will be the driving force behind your actions and decisions, shaping your business's growth and success.

Chapter 11
Bold beliefs

Now, let's reinforce that decision and deal with any negative beliefs we might have about ourselves and our capabilities. We all carry some limiting beliefs, often influenced by external sources like parents, society, or religion. But let's challenge them and create beliefs that truly support us.

Sometimes, fear may creep in, but we can reframe it as excitement about the commitment we've made. Take a deep breath and let's work on aligning our beliefs to empower us on this journey.

Tony Robbins, a master in helping people shape their beliefs and values, once said, "Every decision in your life is controlled by your beliefs and values. You have the power to choose beliefs that empower you towards success." So, let's start by believing we can choose our beliefs to support our goals.

Where do our beliefs come from? Our thoughts, observations of others, stories, experiences, insecurities, and instincts all play a part. Often, we assume beliefs without questioning them. Now is the time to examine our beliefs closely. Don't let the negative self-talk (ego) dictate your journey. As Steve Rizzo puts it, "Tell the big mouth inside your head to shut up."

Let's reframe some common negative beliefs. Instead of seeing self-employment as less secure, consider it as a way to take control of your life and income. Failure is not the end; it's feedback. Time can be managed better if we prioritise our goals. Money is not hard to get; we can set prices that reflect our worth. You get the idea!

The economy may always be uncertain, but your 'personal economy' is different. Growth happens when you step out of your comfort zone. As you commit and take action, your confidence will grow.

You are more than just a teacher; your profession doesn't define your entire identity. Instead, consider a more empowering perspective. You bring out the best in people, nurture talents, and can make a difference in various ways.

Embrace the idea that your current identity doesn't have to be your forever path. Letting go of the familiar can be challenging but essential for aligning with your aspirations and adopting a more empowering identity.

Don't fear letting others down or failing. View your journey as an opportunity to inspire others. By showing them another way, you'll set a positive example.

Shift your mindset from thinking that good things never happen to you. Avoid the victim mindset and focus on progress.

You deserve success and happiness. Acknowledge your self-worth and believe in your right to pursue your dreams, beyond your past.

Your past doesn't determine your future. You have the power to shape your life and create the future you desire. Embrace positive beliefs, challenge negative thoughts, and visualise your success.

Build confidence by taking action, visualising your success, and embracing new opportunities. Strengthen your resilience and protect your energy from negativity.

After identifying and reframing your beliefs, symbolically let go of the negative ones. Write them all down and then tear them up or shred them, signifying that you're leaving them behind and embracing a new perspective.

Old Belief	How It Makes Me Feel	New Belief	How It Makes Me Feel
Example: This is a terrible time to start a business, the economy is in turmoil and no-one has any money.	2/10	This is a great time to start an online business. Everyone is online more than ever before. Global, national, local economies have little impact on our personal economy. Many people have managed to save money during the pandemic, and are looking to spend their money online. Online education is booming as a result and it is the new normal.	9/10
Belief 1:			
Belief 2:			

Gratitude is Golden

Have you ever considered the impact gratitude could have on your journey, even in the realm of creating an incredible tuition business? It's more than just a feel-good concept – it's a game-changer with fascinating ties to neuroscience.

Picture this: when we consciously recognise and appreciate the positives in our lives, it's like a joyous symphony in our brains. Regions associated with reward and pleasure light up, and voilà! Dopamine, the happiness maestro, takes centre stage. This not only boosts our emotional state but also forms a habit of gratitude, making it easier to focus on the sunny side of life and bid farewell to those gloomy vibes.

But gratitude goes beyond just mental perks. It's a brain-rewiring wizard that can dial down the volume on our natural inclination to dwell on the negatives. Our brains, shaped by evolution, tend to spotlight threats and dangers, but gratitude helps us to flip the script. It shifts our focus to the positive - helping us achieve whatever we set our minds to.

Studies link regular gratitude practices to lower stress hormones, reduced anxiety and depression symptoms, and an all-around improved well-being.

To take your gratitude journey to the next level, consider doing a bit of research into Emotional Freedom Technique (EFT). It's a really simple practice that helps you tap away negative emotions, focusing on specific acupressure points, while acknowledging fears and affirming self-acceptance.

This simple activity can help disperse negative feelings and fears; making room for gratitude to flourish.

So, how can you weave gratitude into your daily routine? Keep it simple. Whether it's a mindful moment in the shower, a bedtime ritual with a candle, or jotting down thoughts in a gratitude journal, find what suits you. Embrace simplicity, make gratitude a daily habit, and watch it become a powerful tool for your personal growth and fulfilment.

Chapter 12

Money

As teachers we often have a tough time valuing ourselves and figuring out how to charge for our services. It's partly because of this idea that teaching should be all about self-sacrifice and not making money. We have become conditioned to feel guilty for wanting to earn more.

Denise Duffield-Thomas, my awesome money mindset mentor, highlights how societal conditioning can lead to money-related guilt and discomfort. She encourages us to recognise that it is entirely acceptable to desire financial abundance and to value our skills and knowledge. By embracing the idea that it's okay to want more money, you can begin to break free from limiting beliefs and confidently set fair, professional prices for the valuable education you provide.

Teachers deserve to be compensated fairly for the incredible work they do, and that includes setting prices that reflect their true worth. When you feel good about charging what you're worth, it will boost your confidence and positively impact your teaching. So, let's embrace the idea that wanting more money is okay and start valuing our skillset and experience for the life-changing outcomes they can truly provide! You've put a lot of effort into developing your mindset, your money-mindset is no less important.

By now, you should have a clear vision of where you're

headed, the programme you'll be delivering, and your target audience.

At this stage, your ideas don't have to be set in stone. It's essential to have a solid foundation to work with, and you can always make subtle adjustments along the way. In the words of one of my former coaches, Kane Ramsey: "Practice makes permanent." The mindset work isn't a one-time thing; it's an ongoing journey. Your notes from the previous chapters are invaluable; cherish them and keep referring to them, especially when you're feeling motivated. Make it a habit to regularly review and update your journal as you grow.

Now, let's discuss how to structure your programme. There are various models to consider:

Classic one-to-one model: This involves delivering individual lessons or coaching sessions, either in person or online. While it can be rewarding, keep in mind that it's a time-for-money exchange, and scaling this model might be challenging.

Blended one-to-one model: Here, you combine one-to-one live sessions with self-study online modules. By offering some self-study options, your clients can progress on their own and deepen their understanding during the one-to-one sessions.

Group live lessons model: Similar to the classic one-to-one model, but you teach a group of students together. This allows you to serve more clients simultaneously, but the business still relies heavily on your time.

Hybrid group model: Like the group live lessons model, but you also provide self-study online modules. This allows you to offer more value to the group and reduces your one-to-one time. (This is the model I use and teach my clients, and honestly, I love it)!

Self-study only model: In this model, you package your self-study online modules as a passive product. Clients work through the material independently, and you may offer optional support through email or a community platform.

Each model has its pros and cons, and it's essential to consider your goals, the level of involvement you desire, and the value you can offer your students. You can mix and match these models to create the best fit for your business.

The Money Tree concept

Let's take a moment to consider the money tree concept.

When we build a business, we create different layers. Let's start at the bottom, the roots. These roots are the free content we put out, which is not really free for us because it takes time to create. Content marketing is essential here, where we share stories, posts, and blogs about our journey, passions, and mission.

You can use free resources like Canva to create content. One strategy is to offer a lead magnet, which can be a free download in exchange for their email address.

This helps attract potential customers who resonate with your offerings.

Moving up to the trunk, this is where we introduce low-ticket or passive products, like e-books or guides, typically priced between £10 to £30. These products can help keep you in your customers' minds and establish you as an authority in your field.

The branches represent the medium-ticket products, like live group programmes with recorded elements. This allows you to deliver to many people at once, saving time and effort.

The medium ticket offer can be a great starting point, and you can repurpose parts of it for free content or even a low-ticket download. You can offer a higher level of personalisation through adding some one-on-one access to you for a high-ticket experience, too. This is the sweet spot we seek to achieve with the 2-Hour Tutor model.

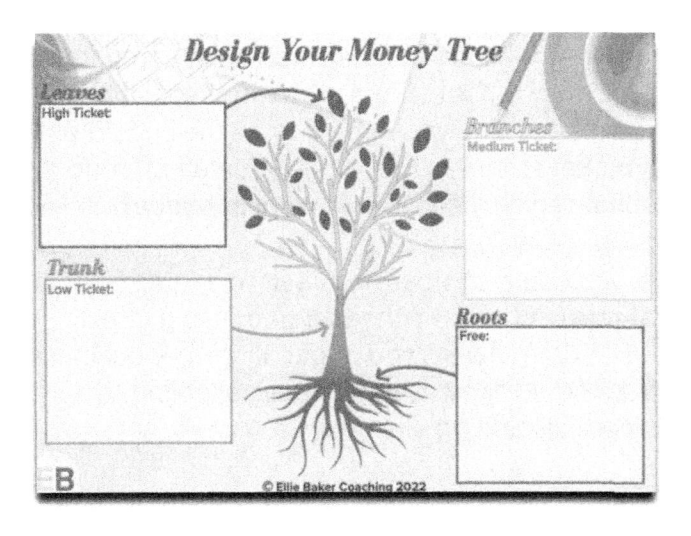

Design Your Money Tree

Leaves
High Ticket:

Branches
Medium Ticket:

Trunk
Low Ticket:

Roots
Free:

© Ellie Baker Coaching 2022

Pricing your services

Let's dive deeper into the topic of pricing and explore the key factors you need to consider when determining the right price for your offering. Remember, the goal is to position yourself strategically and communicate the value you provide to your target audience.

Imagine you're running a language teaching business, focusing on helping semi-retired expats in Spain become fluent in Spanish. These potential clients have been struggling for years with language barriers, which have caused them financial losses, social isolation, and a lack of confidence. Your mission is to empower them to overcome these challenges and lead a rich, fulfilling life in their new home.

Now, when setting your price, it's essential to avoid pricing by asking around your friends or basing it on what competitors charge. Instead, think about where you want to position yourself in the market. Are you aiming to be the budget option like a mass-market store, or do you see yourself offering high-quality, personalised services like a luxury boutique?

For instance, you could compare yourself to a retail chain like Asda (or Walmart) that offers cheaper goods to a large customer base. Alternatively, you might align your business with a premium brand like Anthropologie, appealing to a smaller but more discerning clientele.

Once you've chosen your positioning, you need to quantify the value you provide. Shift the focus away from the product itself and emphasise the outcomes your clients can expect. For your language teaching business, highlight the life-changing benefits of speaking Spanish fluently: improved relationships with family and friends, increased confidence, and enhanced opportunities to fully immerse in Spanish culture.

By clearly defining the specific group of people you want to serve, you can create a more compelling message tailored to their needs. For example, in your marketing, speak directly to the expats who have struggled with language barriers and showcase how your tuition programme addresses their pain points directly.

Remember, you're not just selling language lessons; you're selling the transformation and the long-term impact on their lives. By focusing on the end result, you can justify a higher price point, and your potential clients will recognise the value of investing in themselves. They'll understand that the price they pay is an investment in their future happiness and fulfilment.

Business coach Marie Folio uses a mattress analogy to demonstrate the same point. Just as she focuses on the comfort, support, and quality of the mattress rather than its price tag, you should concentrate on the value your language teaching programme offers. Make it clear that your services are worth the investment, and that the benefits they'll gain far outweigh the cost.

Have you ever come across the tale of Picasso and the napkin? According to legend, while at a Paris market, Picasso was approached by an admirer who requested a swift sketch on a paper napkin.

Agreeing gracefully, Picasso quickly knocked up a beautiful

drawing of a bird and returned the napkin — but not without asking for 300 francs.

The lady was taken aback, exclaiming, "It only took you five minutes to draw this!" Picasso replied, "No, it took me 40 years to draw this in just five minutes."

This anecdote should deeply resonate - your subject knowledge and teaching skill is a craft that has been honed over the course of years, decades, even!

Strategic pricing involves positioning yourself in the market, quantifying the value you provide, and effectively communicating the transformative outcomes you offer. By being exclusive in your target market and emphasising the long-term impact on your clients' lives, you can justify higher prices and attract those who truly value what you have to offer. Pricing is not just about numbers; it's about communicating the lifelong worth and impact of your services.

Check out these examples of how you can structure your pricing and number of students to achieve your desired income level:

Katie's Fitness Programme:

As a former PE teacher with a new baby, Katie had a vision of helping new mums regain their fitness while balancing her own life. She knew there was a demand for postnatal fitness programmes, and she decided to capitalise on it. Starting with six clients for 8 weeks, and charging £300 each, this allowed her to manage her time effectively and offer personalised attention to each participant. She carefully planned her programme along with her first cohort, ensuring it provided value and delivered results. This experience brought her £1800, which had to last her 2 months. Not a bad start!

Initially, Katie was hesitant to charge too much, as she was unsure of how her clients would respond. However, as she gained experience and positive feedback, she also gained confidence in her abilities. This newfound courage led her to raise her rates and take on more clients. With ten clients at £500 each, she is generating a higher income of £2500 per month while still providing an excellent service. She is now considering a rolling enrolment approach; whereby new clients can be added to the programme at any time. She is confident that her video content will guide new clients sufficiently, and that they will benefit from joining weekly zoom calls with those who are further down the line.

Andy's 11 Plus Tutoring:

Andy, a seasoned teacher with extensive experience in 11 plus tutoring, recognised the market demand for high-quality tutoring services. He knew he had the skills and expertise to help students excel in their exams. Deciding to start with four clients at £500 each allowed him to devote ample time to each student, ensuring they received personalised attention.

Andy's initial pricing decision was influenced by his perception of the value he offered. He wanted to offer a competitive rate, yet one that reflected the quality of his services. As he saw the positive impact his tutoring had on his clients, he realised the value he brought and was more confident in raising his rates for future clients. If he could reach his goal of taking on 5 new students per month at £600, he would be able to fully replace his teaching salary teaching just 2 hours per week.

As both Katie and Andy continued their businesses, they adapted their strategies based on experience and feedback. They identified the right balance between the number of clients they could handle, the quality of service they wanted to provide, and the income they desired. By staying flexible and open to changes, they were able to achieve their financial goals and build thriving businesses.

Key Takeaways:

1. Know your niche and target audience: Understanding your target market and the value you bring to them is crucial for setting the right pricing and delivering a successful product or service.

2. Confidence and value: Confidence in your skills and the value you provide is vital for determining appropriate pricing. Don't undervalue yourself; if you offer the desired outcomes, the right clients will be willing to pay for it.

3. Start small and scale up: Starting with a manageable number of clients allows you to fine-tune your programme and gain confidence. As you gain experience and positive feedback, you can scale up and adjust your pricing accordingly.

Have a play with the numbers yourself. Remember, there's no right or wrong with pricing. You can go higher or lower based on your value and target audience. Just ensure your pricing aligns with your goals and desired income.

Picasso's napkin

Doing the numbers exercise might have either left you a bit overwhelmed, or it might have made you feel uncomfortable about setting prices and asking for money. I want to reassure you that those numbers are just examples to show how you could structure your business and pricing.

I purposely challenge my teacher clients to start a bit on the high end, so you have room to adjust and feel more comfortable. However, I encourage you not to undersell yourself and to set a price that feels a bit higher than what you're used to.

We need to move away from the hourly rate mindset. Charging by the hour devalues us and leads to price comparisons based on the market. Instead, I want you to focus on creating a package or an experience that provides real value and results for your students.

Consider the lifetime value of the solution you're offering. Think about the lasting impact of your teachings on their lives and the potential cost of not taking your course. You have years of training, experience, and teaching skills that add incredible value to what you offer.

Just like Picasso's napkin, it may seem like your expertise only takes a short time to deliver, but it's the culmination of your lifetime of experience that truly makes it valuable.

So, think big and outside the traditional hourly rates. Create a programme that delivers immense value and transforms your clients' lives. You're worth it, and your unique teaching approach will make your course stand out from the rest. Remember, you have the power to create something that far surpasses other offerings in the market.

Embrace your worth and the confidence will come with it!

Pricing and our emotions

Now, let's take a closer look at some different price points and how they make you feel.

Imagine yourself charging these prices, starting with £15,000. No judgements, just notice your emotions.

Consider the kind of person you'd be serving, their lifestyle, and the problems they need solving. What's your solution for them?

Next, let's talk about £9,000. Personally, I've paid that price for a three-month course, and it was a no-brainer. Exactly what I needed, with incredible results. No regrets whatsoever.

Now, picture offering a three or six-month program to a client at this price point. How does that sit with you?

Moving on, what about £1,197 for a three-month programme, (equivalent to about a hundred pounds per week)? How does that price feel to you?

Think about the elements you'd include to make it a compelling value offering.

Now, let's discuss 97 pounds. For me, at this price, I'd probably offer a DIY mini-course. Useful, but nowhere near as impactful as live group work.

The more you charge, the more commitment you're likely to get from your students, and the better the results they will achieve. This produces a beautiful 'upwards spiral' of results, reviews for your programme, more clients, greater value, and justified price increases for your services. The value you want to provide should align with the price you set.

In my experience, the nine grand course made the most significant impact, followed by the £1,197 programme. At 9k I was determined to make my money back quickly - so I followed the programme to the letter - resulting in me recouping twice my investment shortly after completing the course (the outcome for your students need not be monetary, just tangible and clear).

The 97-pound downloads, on the other hand, weren't as life-changing. It's important to consider the value you're delivering at different price points.

> Take a moment to reflect on your own experiences with various price ranges and the outcomes they brought into your life. It's an insightful exercise to consider. Feel free to pause and think about how your investments have translated into results.

Dream Big

We've already taken some time to sit with the numbers and explore how they make us feel. It's fascinating how money triggers so much within us, especially when we've been working for low pay rates. We need to shift that mindset.

To determine our prices, we should follow a reverse-engineered process. Start by asking yourself: How much money do you want to earn? What kind of lifestyle do you desire? Do you want to own a house, travel the world, or have more time for your kids? Your purpose and driving force behind your financial goals are crucial.

Don't be afraid to want more from life. It's okay to desire luxury, better living conditions, or more time for yourself. Let go of any limiting beliefs that hold you back. Give yourself permission to want what you truly desire.

Consider creating a dream board or a Pinterest board, visualising your ideal car, house, and other aspirations. Embrace the idea of dedicating your time and resources to give back to the world once you achieve your financial goals.

Remember, you don't need external validation to pursue your dreams. Give yourself permission and work on clearing any money blocks, guilt, or fear you may have. Look up Denise Duffield Thomas for inspiration and practical guidance on money matters.

Dream big, and believe in yourself. You've got this!

Which person do you want to be - Rochelle or Lucy?

In this section, I want to share a powerful analogy with you. This triggers strong emotions in me. It reminds me of the time when I felt buried under the responsibilities of being a school teacher!

Let's explore two different scenarios:

Person A, let's call her Rochelle, runs a tuition business charging £25 per hour, teaching languages to students. To live comfortably, she needs 20 hours of tuition per week. On the surface, it looks good, as she could potentially earn £500 a week with 20 hours of tuition.

But in reality, there are weeks and months without earnings due to holidays or cancelled sessions. Some students don't pay on time, making it challenging for Rochelle to manage her finances. At the end of the year, after taxes, she struggles to make ends meet. She ends up working more than 20 hours, and the stress of uncertainty and demanding parents takes a toll on her.

Now, let's meet Person B, Lucy. She teaches German and has a completely different approach. Lucy designs a 12-week beginner's course, providing recorded videos and a digital workbook for her students. She targets a specific audience – adults who are retired and have time during the day. She charges £80 per week for her programme.

With just six people in her group, Lucy earns £5,760 for the 12-week programme. Her contact time is minimal, spending only about one hour per week on live Zoom sessions and a few hours for emails and feedback. Lucy has built a strong community around her course, and her clients enjoy the social interaction in the group.

Comparing the two scenarios, it's clear that Lucy's approach provides a better experience for her clients. They get a structured programme, ongoing support, and a collaborative community, making them more likely to achieve their goals.

The key lesson here is that it's not just about the money; it's about delivering value and serving your ideal clients effectively. When you provide a solution that meets their needs and aligns with their desires, the money will follow naturally.

So, before you decide on your teaching or coaching model, think deeply about who you want to serve and how you can best deliver value to them. Focus on creating a programme that resonates with your ideal clients, and you'll see better results and happier customers. It's a win-win!

Final thoughts on money mindset

Remember, working on our money mindset is like exercising a muscle. We need to put effort into it and reinforce the positive beliefs we want to hold about money.

For example, some people may think tutors only charge £30 per hour, which can lead to unhelpful beliefs. But we can challenge this thought with logic and create a positive mindset booster. Like realising that hourly rates can lead to burnouts, while packages offer a win-win situation for both parties.

Think of a role model who follows this model successfully and admire their approach. Let that influence guide your beliefs.

CASE STUDY

From maths teacher to building a successful business – meet Tom Hawkins.

Name: Tom Hawkins

Business: Tom Hawkins Education (Maths Tuition)

Website: www.tomhawkinseducation.com

Problem: Didn't want to return to classroom teaching after taking some time out to travel.

Success: He now has more time to spend with his family and has discovered his true potential.

Before working with Ellie...

After 4 years in the secondary maths classroom, Tom was taking some time out of his career to travel and spend more time with his family when he started looking for support with setting up his own maths tuition business...

When he first hopped on board the 2-Hour Tutor programme, he was faced with either returning to the classroom or carving out a new path that would allow him more quality time with his family.

One thing was missing, however – he lacked a clear roadmap to make a success of his online tutoring business. He was keen to adopt a time-leveraged group model, knowing that it would give him the time flexibility he craved without losing out on income.

The information overload out there had his head spinning, and he just wanted someone he could trust to point him in the right direction.

He started researching different programmes and spoke to a few other coaches, but decided that the 2-hour tutor programme was ideal both from a personality fit and learning perspective.

Fast forward 6 months...

Fast forward 6 months, and his experience with the 2-Hour Tutor programme has been a real game-changer. He's now reaping the rewards of his efforts is and loving every bit of the new lifestyle he has created for himself.

As Tom puts it, "It's been a bit of a rollercoaster for me." Initially, he wasn't sure about the investment for the programme, but with a little nudge of encouragement from his brother, he took the plunge. Now, he sees it as a small investment for the kind of lifestyle he's building.

In this interview Tom talks about the programme's five pillars, which cover everything from running an online business and marketing to personal growth.

According to Tom, these pillars are essential to succeed in the online education world. "You've got to have all of those things to be successful," he says.

Tom doesn't sugarcoat it, though. He admits that the programme requires hard work. But he believes the payoff is more than worth it: "You'll get that back tenfold, hundredfold." He encourages anyone on the fence to take the leap, saying, "I don't think you can *not* join."

Looking ahead, Tom's keeping his options open. He's realised that the programme isn't just about business but also personal development. As he puts it, "It's been more about learning what my limitations were, my own strengths and weaknesses." He's excited about what the future holds, even if it's not all neatly planned out.

So, in Tom's words, "I wouldn't think twice about joining . . . you're worth it."

Tom's story is a testament to how the 2-Hour Tutor programme can help you not only build a thriving online education business but also discover your whole life's potential along the way.

Another common thought that might come up is feeling less experienced than others. But remember, pricing isn't about experience; it's about the perception of value you offer. Embrace the mindset booster that acknowledges your ability to teach anything, and that fresh knowledge can sometimes make you a better teacher.

Find a role model who pivoted from one career to another successfully, even with limited experience, and let their story inspire you.

Lastly, don't worry about what others might say or think about your pricing. Focus on serving the right audience, and don't let external opinions dictate your decisions.

As you work on your money mindset, consider decluttering any triggers that affect you, whether it's certain social media, people, or things in your environment.

Remember, this is an ongoing process, but if you commit to it and do the work, it will definitely pay off. You don't want to go back to where you started. So enjoy the process and see you in the next chapter!

Chapter 13

Choose your niche

I used to hate marketing, especially when I was a teacher. It seemed like something only slimy salespeople did. But then, I had an "aha" moment when I realised that even as a teacher, I was doing marketing stuff. Running open evenings and pushing for more pupils to opt for a language GCSE— that's marketing and sales right there!

I totally disagree with the idea that teachers can't pick up these skills in a way that feels right for them. Teachers are some of the smartest, most adaptable people I know. That's why I love working with you all. You can totally learn this stuff, and trust me, it's not that hard. If you can teach, you can pretty much do anything in my book. And if I can do it, so can you! Let's get into it and up your marketing game together.

First thing's first - we need to define our ideal client:

This is an exciting process that fleshes out the person we want to serve. We don't want to serve just anyone, but rather a specific type of person with particular needs and preferences.

Defining our ideal client is a crucial step because it helps us create a niche for ourselves. We want to be specialists, not generalists. By understanding our ideal client deeply, we can step into their shoes and truly understand their world.

We will go deep in this chapter, exploring how they see the world, how they live day-to-day, their thoughts, fears, hobbies, shopping preferences, and more. We'll give them a name, an age or age bracket, and really get to know them on a personal level.

The reason we do this is to create a targeted program that delivers specific results to a specific audience. Having a niche makes our offer easier to sell and allows us to provide more value to our clients.

Feel free to journal your ideas as you work through this chapter, and remember that this is a crucial step to set the foundation for your successful business.

Don't most parents just want 1:1 tuition for their kids?

We've all heard the common objections: "Isn't one-to-one better value?" "Is one-to-one more efficient and personalised for my child?" "Surely, one-to-one is the superior choice?"

If you've ever pondered these questions or struggled to articulate the advantages of group programmes (even to yourself!), then you're in for a treat. We're here to dispel these myths and shed light on the true potential of group tuition.

Let's be clear – not all group programmes are created equal. We understand that some may conjure images of generic Zoom sessions with a multitude of kids, which can understandably raise concerns.

However, when meticulously crafted and effectively communicated to our ideal clients, which are the parents and their children, group programmes can be a game-changer.

So, let's dive into 6 of the most common myths and FAQs we hear at the 2-Hour Tutor HQ. Feel free to use them yourself if the need arises!

6 of the most common myths and FAQs

Q: Isn't one-to-one tuition more personalised?

A: While one-to-one tuition can provide individual attention, it can also lead to an over-reliance on the weekly meetings with the tutor and, ultimately, slow progress. Group tuition, when structured well, is built with 3 core pillars:

> 1 – Self-study. Students can access a pre-recorded curriculum in the form of video content meaning valuable lesson time isn't wasted, and is more productive
>
> 2 – One to one feedback. Students can reach out to their tutor between lessons if they don't understand something, and tutors give personalised feedback using efficient tools such as screen recording and voice notes, so that they can continue to progress between lessons.
>
> 3 – Group learning. Students can share their perspectives on the learning and go deeper with their tutor, meaning progress is made faster.

1:1 tuition, on the other hand, lacks these elements and all the focus is in the allocated lesson time, which can be inefficient and stressful (see below).

Q: My child is already resistant to having a tutor. Won't a group setting make it worse?

A: In fact, the reverse can often be true. The intense focus required for 1:1 tuition can be stressful for both the tutor and the student. Additionally, the gap between lessons is typically quite long, which can result in poor retention of information and a loss of learning efficiency.

Q: Why is group learning better for children?

A: Children (and even adults) often thrive when they are among their peers, as they can relate to and learn from each other. Group learning fosters interaction, collaboration, and socialisation. It also allows for more opportunities to engage in enjoyable activities and switching things up with games and breakout rooms, which have been proven to facilitate learning.

Q: How does group learning work?

A: Our courses are designed to combine group learning with individualised attention. Students access video lessons weekly, taking ownership of their learning and preparing for the group sessions. We also provide a direct line of communication between the tutor and the student, encouraging them to reach out with questions and submit work for review.

This way, progress can be made both individually and as part of the group learning experience. The result is that much more progress is made week on week when compared to the 1:1 tuition where progress can be much slower.

Q: Is 1:1 tuition better value than a group programme?

A: It's a common misconception that one-to-one tuition offers better value than a group programme. In reality, 1:1 tuition fees can range from £30 to £50 per hour or even more, depending on the specialisation.

If you consider having these sessions every week for an indefinite period, which could be as long as an entire academic year or more, it can add up to £2000 plus.

This doesn't include travel expenses for face-to-face sessions, nor the hidden costs of lack of retention between sessions. On the other hand, a well-crafted group programme with a specialised teacher typically ranges from £400 to £800, offering not only cost savings but also saving time.

In just 12 weeks or even less, children can overcome their challenges and get back to excelling in their studies while regaining time for their hobbies and social activities.

Q: Isn't face-to-face learning better than online learning?

A: While face-to-face learning may have some benefits of physical presence, the advantages of online learning outweigh the drawbacks. Firstly, as a parent, you eliminate the need for driving time and fuel costs by opting for online learning.

Your child can comfortably have their lessons at home, and you can even be in the same room or nearby, ensuring they are engaged and supported throughout. Moreover, online learning offers flexibility in scheduling and removes geographical barriers.

It also provides access to a wider pool of expert tutors, expanding the options available to your child. Don't worry, the online format doesn't compromise the quality of education or support your child receives.

The keyword here is "educate." As educators, it's our duty to educate our audience on the merits of well-designed group tuition programmes. Only then can people truly appreciate the differences.

Many have not experienced a well-crafted group programme, and it's our task to explain why this isn't just the best and most fun option for their child but also the most efficient and cost-effective one in the long run.

If you've found it challenging to convey these benefits to potential parents then the above FAQ list should help!

What are they thinking?

Let's go deeper into the thoughts of your ideal student (or their parents)! We know who they are, where they hang out, and what they like doing. But can we delve further into what they truly want to fix, which you can help them with?

What is their perspective on the problem? What spinoff problems arise in their lives due to this issue? Imagine their dream life if you could help them achieve it or remove the obstacle blocking their path.

For example, if it's a parent wanting to fix something for their child, like struggling with maths, what are their worries if this problem goes unfixed? How does it affect their confidence and school choices, and their future prospects as a whole?

If possible, talk to someone in a similar situation, or even use your imagination to write a diary entry from your ideal client's perspective. Capture their pain, struggles, and desires related to the problem.

Your personal story should answer why they should choose you. Focus on how you can quickly and painlessly get them from where they are (point A) to where they want to be (point B). Keep it concise and engaging, less is definitely more when it comes to writing marketing copy.

Your Ideal Client Avatar

Now let's dive into defining your Ideal Client Avatar or ICA. Now, marketing can seem complicated, so let's simplify it. Marketing is about finding people who fit your ICA and nurturing them. Think of it as creating and building a relationship with a pool of ideal clients over time.

Imagine your pool of people, your ICA, as a lake.

We want to fill this lake with happy fish who are ready to take the next step with you. So how do we do that?

Content is key.

Content builds relationships, and relationships are built on trust. Trust drives revenue.

Your content should be focused on helping your ideal clients. Offer them valuable tips and insights related to your course subject. Make them feel understood and supported. Remember, people won't forget how you make them feel.

Now, where do we hold this lake of happy fish? You can do it through various means, but one effective method is creating a private Facebook group. It's a great way to nurture your audience and offer them free content. Later, when you're ready to launch your course, you can create a separate group for those who've purchased it.

Of course, the approach may vary depending on your personality type. If you're a community-builder, the Facebook group option may suit you well. If you're an analyst, a PDF download with valuable, free content and an invite to book a call with you might be more effective.

The key is to keep it simple, genuine, and aligned with who you are. Building your pool of ideal clients takes time, but it's a valuable asset for when you're ready to make your offer. So remember, content builds relationships, and relationships drive revenue. Focus on helping and nurturing your audience, and you'll see the results over time.

Now you can link accounts, making it easier and quicker to get your posts on several platforms. You can link your Facebook to post on Twitter and Instagram.

You may want to consider, if you're quite techy and confident with social media, getting an account with HootSuite. It's free and you can post to multiple channels, but more importantly, you can tweak it for each channel. For example, Instagram is all about the hashtags, while with Facebook, it looks spammy to use hashtags. You could use one or two at most, but on Instagram, you can hashtag the hell out of everything.

Now, if you're not into Instagram, don't worry. It's not really my thing either. Facebook, however, is a no-brainer. There's so much you can do with it.

If you're targeting business people, for example - stressed working mums in the corporate world, then LinkedIn would be a good place for you. It's brilliant for professional discussions and conversations.

Consider where your ICA (Ideal Customer Avatar) hangs out. If they're over 60, they probably won't be on Instagram. Most people are on Facebook anyway. If your course is interest-based, not very work-related, creating a Facebook group is a good idea. Business pages have less reach on Facebook, but groups can be nurturing and rewarding.

If the thought of managing a social media group makes you feel uneasy, work on any blocks or imposter syndrome you may have.

Alternatively, if you're time-poor or introverted, consider running targeted Facebook ads. They can lead potential customers to your lead magnet or webinar, helping you build your email list.

Take the time to think about what's best for you. Choose a

strategy that aligns with your personality and doesn't drain you. Later on, we'll work together on a content plan, making it easy for you to engage with your group or audience.

By mastering a specific marketing style, it becomes easier to measure results and make improvements. It's much better than trying everything and not knowing what's working.

In the past, I made the mistake of not having a clear marketing strategy, just posting randomly on Facebook, Instagram, and Twitter. But doing something is better than nothing, right?

Focus on one thing that resonates with your values, attracting people who are like you. It's about going for the low-hanging fruit and not trying to appeal to everyone.

No more comparing yourself to others. Embrace your uniqueness and use authenticity as your strength to market your business effectively.

Remember, don't rush into anything just yet. Take the time to consider what will work best for you as your next step.

Planning Your Customer Journey

So now you've learned quite a bit about marketing, whether you were already familiar with some concepts or they were entirely new to you.

Next, we'll be moving on to designing your customer journey. This is often referred to as a funnel, and it's a good word to describe the process. Think of it like getting people's attention first, building a relationship, sparking their interest, and ultimately leading them to take action and become your customers.

The key is to get the attention of the right people who fit your ideal client, rather than just trying to attract everyone. For example, having a Facebook page with a lot of likes from friends and family who won't actually engage with your content may not be helpful. Instead, focus on genuinely interested people who will interact with your posts.

To begin, we create awareness through social media or other channels, directing people to a 'lead magnet'—a free resource such as a PDF download that captures their email address. Once they become prospects, we nurture the relationship by providing valuable content and making offers. Not everyone will buy, and that's okay. The goal is to have enough prospects in the funnel to generate customers.

You can keep it simple by using Facebook or other platforms to lead prospects to your lead magnet, and then provide a link to book a call with you.

Instead of calling it a funnel, I prefer the term "customer journey" because it's like bringing people on a journey to fall in love with what you offer. You can draw out your customer journey in any way you like, using arrows, bullets, or a simplified model like the one I've shared.

Now, it's your turn to design your customer journey. You can use the image provided or freestyle it as you like. Don't worry about the complexity; just keep it simple and clear.

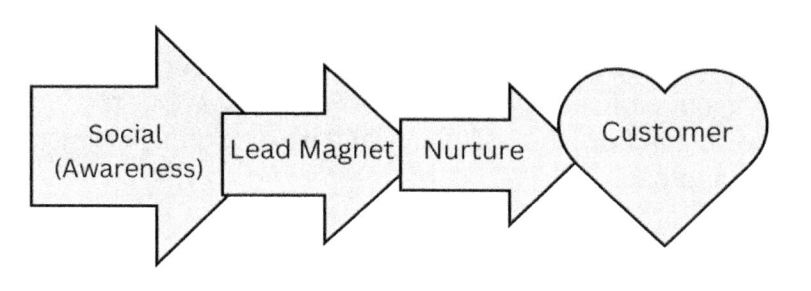

Social (Awareness) → Lead Magnet → Nurture → Customer

Chapter 14

Cracking Content

This chapter is where we, as teachers, come into our own: designing our course outline. Some of you may have been eager to do this from the beginning, and we're taking a slightly different approach.

We've instead started by considering our customer, working on our money mindset, and planning our income. Instead of just looking at hourly rates, we've explored various income scenarios and package options.

All the groundwork we've done will help us move forward, allowing us to be more creative and thoughtful about the customer we're serving when creating the course. It might seem easy now since we've been thinking about it for a while, identifying our target audience, where they hang out, and how we'll market ourselves to reach them.

Remember, the name of the course isn't something to stress about right now. Brainstorm a few ideas without settling on one immediately. When recording or preparing course materials, it's best not to use the course name unless you're absolutely certain about it. The name should clearly convey the results you're offering, avoiding anything too elusive or vague.

Now, let's move on to designing the course outline. We'll start by determining the end result we want to achieve for our students. This results-driven approach will guide us in planning out the journey. I find it helpful to visualise the end result and work backward to identify the necessary steps.

Choosing a format for the course can be flexible, but I prefer the one module per week approach. It's easier to keep track of where each student is in their learning process. However, you can adjust the number of weeks or steps based on your audience and their needs.

This is the fun part - the creative phase. Embrace your personality and experiences as a teacher. It's an opportunity to bring all your knowledge and unique insights into the course.

For practical tools, a Google Doc works great for organising ideas and inspirations. You can even access it from your phone as well as from your desktop. Alternatively, if you're more visual, consider using Trello, a free app that allows you to arrange and organise information like virtual post-it notes.

Keep in mind that the core process is understanding your students' pain points and guiding them to a place of happiness, accomplishment, and fulfilment by the end of the course.

Enjoy mapping out this journey!

Attracting ideal students

Now that you have a course outline and an ideal customer in mind, we can move on to producing a free piece of content to attract them into your world. This is often referred to as a 'lead magnet' (I prefer the term 'read' magnet)!

It doesn't have to be a PDF; it can be an audio file or a video instead. The goal is to provide real value quickly and entice your audience to take further action.

Don't be afraid to give away valuable content for free. The lead magnet should be irresistible, offering a specific solution to a problem in exchange for their contact information. Keep it simple and easy to consume, as nobody wants to go through lengthy videos or read long reports.

Here are some title ideas: "10 Strategies to Help You XXX," "Survival Guide for XXX," "Essential Guide to XXX," or "How to XXX Without XXX."

When designing your lead magnet, remember it doesn't have to be complex; just solve a specific problem that you know your audience struggles with by providing a specific solution. Don't try to solve all their problems at once, and don't overthink branding at this stage; two colours and two fonts will do. Canva is a great tool to help you design it quickly and easily.

Narrow your focus, choose one idea, and get it done. Remember, done is better than perfect. It's all about providing value and attracting your ideal clients. You can always improve and refine later. Don't get overwhelmed; just take action.

You can sign up for mine to see how it works here: elliebakereducation.com/2hr-tutor-blueprint.

What next for my lead magnet?

Before you take any next steps, you'll want to set up a 'professional' email address with a domain name for your new business. Once you've set this up, you can sign up to a free email service provider, such as Mailerlite, which allows you to easily add people to your mail list using some canny automation tools that require some initial setup.

For instance, when someone signs up for your lead magnet, Mailerlite will send them a professional-looking email with your free content automatically, making your life a lot easier (and meaning you can deliver your content to eager prospects while you sleep)!

As your list grows, you'll want to set up workflows to manage your subscribers. This will help you stay organised and ensure that everyone receives timely communication from you. With software such as Mailerlite, you can create workflows easily, ensuring a smooth and automated process for delivering content to your audience.

So, to sum it up, setting up an email service provider like Flodesk (my favourite) or MailerLite is an essential step in your journey. Once you overcome this hurdle, you'll be well-prepared to start properly marketing your business in the most efficient way possible. Get this done and then you'll be ready to move forward with attracting ideal clients for your business!

Chapter 15

Review and Practicalities to consider

Congratulations! You've already done half of the work. The hard thinking, planting seeds, and clearing clutter are behind you. Now, you'll start reaping the rewards of your foundational work.

We've made significant progress – from working on mindset to defining our audience, mission, and course outline. Plus, we've created a lead magnet to attract people. Many people overlook these critical steps, but not you!

Moving forward, we'll dive into practicalities, such as timeline and financial planning. We'll discuss technology and systems, including email service providers and payment options. Then, we'll focus on selling and social media strategies tailored to your preferences.

Copywriting skills are crucial too. We'll learn how to write engaging posts and sales pages without sounding 'salesy.' And when you're ready, we'll cover the process of launching your business.

Remember the daily standards we set at the beginning? Keep upholding them! Stay mindful of your thoughts and beliefs, and avoid letting negative influences hinder your progress.

Reverse-engineer your plan

Imagine you've achieved your goal. You're a few months down the line, running your successful programme, with clients seeking access to it. You've left your previous teaching role (or you've moved away from intensive 1:1 tuition) and can see that everything is working out.

Feel the excitement of sitting at your desk, about to log on to Zoom and meet your lovely group. Now, think about how you accomplished this goal. What commitments did you make? What hurdles did you overcome? Who supported you along the way? Consider the systems and technology that helped you achieve success.

By visualising your future success, you're building the belief that it's possible. Remember Henry Ford's famous saying, "If you think you can or you think you can't, you're right." So, imprint this belief in your mind. It makes you mindful of what you need to do to get there.

Let's take Andy as an example. He's an 11 plus tutor who's made significant progress. He's connected with his ideal clients, outlined his course, and gathered a decent email list. Offering free workshops has helped him spread the word and grow his authority. Now, he plans to create a Facebook group and run regular workshops to expand his audience further. He's confident about the future and sees the potential to continuously enrol new students, making a steady income.

Your next step is to create a plan of action. What steps did you take to get to where you are in your future vision? Write them down in order (or reverse order, if you find it easier to work backwards)!

Whether you prefer a simple table or a more structured approach, get into the mindset of your future self. Feel the excitement and own that feeling; it will fuel your belief and motivation to take the necessary steps towards your goal.

Good luck with the exercise, and enjoy the journey towards achieving your dreams!

Finances

Let's talk about finances. I want to clarify that I'm not a financial guru, nor do I have any qualifications in finance. But I've managed my own money for most of my adult life, and since becoming self-employed in 2013, I've learned quite a bit.

First, when you start earning money from your business, consider registering as self-employed with HMRC, probably within the first three months. You can be self-employed and employed simultaneously. If your earnings are below around £13k per year, you won't have to pay income tax, but you may need to pay some National Insurance contributions.

Deciding between being a sole trader or a limited company depends on your preferences and circumstances. Becoming a sole trader is simpler to set up and manage, while a limited company can offer some tax benefits and limited liability. Speak to an accountant or someone familiar with small business needs to get the right advice.

VAT is not a concern unless your earnings exceed around £80,000 per year, so don't worry about it in the early stages. Keep a basic spreadsheet of your income and expenses, and make sure you open a separate business bank account to keep things organised.

As for saving, I recommend setting aside about 25% of your income to cover taxes and other unexpected expenses. It's a good practice to start early to avoid any last-minute surprises.

Remember that HMRC is moving towards monthly tax bills in the future, so saving regularly will be beneficial.

While HMRC rarely scrutinises small businesses like ours, it's essential to keep your records in order and be transparent about your finances. Having a separate bank account and basic financial records will make your life easier when dealing with taxes and financial planning.

Remember, I'm not a financial expert, but I hope these insights will help you on your financial journey. You can seek some initial free advice from an accountant or a financial advisor for personalised advice.

How do I protect myself as a business owner?

When it comes to running a business in the UK and the European Union, there's an essential thing you need to know about – the General Data Protection Regulation, or simply GDPR. Don't let the name scare you; it's all about protecting people's privacy and personal data.

So, what does GDPR mean for you as a tuition business owner? Well, it's pretty simple – you should only collect the data you actually need from your customers. There's no need to ask for their favourite ice cream flavour unless you're planning to send them a sweet surprise!

To play it safe and stay on the good side of GDPR, you'll want to have a clear and honest privacy policy on your website. Tell your customers what data you're collecting, why you're collecting it, and how you're going to protect it. If you're using cookies (the digital kind, not the chocolate chip ones!) make sure to let your visitors know and explain how they're used.

Now, let's chat about protecting your awesome ideas! If you've come up with a brilliant logo for your business, you're already covered by copyright protection. It means your creative work is protected from the moment you put it out there in the world – no need to fill out any forms or jump through hoops.

But hey, why not sprinkle a little extra magic on it? You can show off your copyright-protected work by putting the © symbol next to your name and the year it was created.

When it comes to your brand, you'll want to give it some extra love and attention. That's where trademarks come into play. A trademark can be your business name, logo, or even a catchy slogan that sets you apart from the crowd, giving your brand an identity of its own.

To get the full protection for your brand, you can register your trademark with the UK Intellectual Property Office or the European Union Intellectual Property Office. It's like putting a powerful shield around your brand, so no one else can use it without your permission.

Drawing up some clear and comprehensive terms and

conditions for your tutoring services is of utmost importance for several reasons:

- Legal protection: Terms and conditions serve as a legally binding agreement between you and your users. They outline the rights and responsibilities of both parties, reducing the risk of disputes and potential legal issues.
- User understanding: By providing clear terms and conditions, you ensure that your users are fully aware of the rules and guidelines governing the use of your tutoring programme. This helps to avoid misunderstandings and sets expectations for a smooth user experience.
- Liability limitation: Including disclaimers and liability clauses in your terms and conditions can protect you from certain types of claims, such as inaccuracies in the content provided or any issues arising from third-party links.
- Data protection and privacy: Terms and conditions should outline how user data is collected, used, and protected. Ensuring compliance with data protection laws builds trust and credibility with your users.
- Payment and refund policies: Clear terms on payment methods, charges, and refund procedures help manage financial transactions and prevent potential payment disputes.
- Intellectual property rights: If tutors provide original content, it is essential to outline how intellectual property rights are handled to avoid potential conflicts over ownership and usage.
- Updates and modifications: Having a section that explains how and when the terms and conditions may be updated provides transparency and keeps users informed about changes to the platform's policies.

Having well-defined terms and conditions protects your tutoring website, enhances user trust, and contributes to a positive user experience, thereby supporting the long-term success of your platform. While there are low-cost plug and play templates out there you can use, it is recommended to seek legal advice to ensure that your terms and conditions comply with relevant laws and regulations.

Remember, while you can handle all of this on your own, it's totally okay to ask for a little help from experts in the field.

They'll guide you through the process, so you can focus on what you do best – teaching!

Chapter 16

Tech and social media

Welcome to this chapter where we'll delve into technology and how it can benefit you. Perhaps you've already done some research or set up an email account, which is great.

Let me introduce you to 'the simple tech stack'. A tech stack is simply a system composed of various technological components that work together to reach and engage your customers, from the first introduction to providing them with valuable content.

Now, let's explore the technology that can make this process smooth and efficient.

Level 1 tech stack

Meet Suzy, who's chosen a free and basic level one tech stack.

Step one is making sure customers know about you, essentially - marketing. Suzy uses social media, specifically Facebook and Instagram, along with her lead magnet, to attract people to step two—the landing page.

The landing page is where Suzy captures visitors' email

addresses, first names, and last names, along with any other relevant information. She'll use Mailerlite, which provides a landing page feature, so she doesn't need a separate website.

Once people sign up on her landing page, Mailerlite's automatic responder will send them the link to download Suzy's lead magnet, which can be a PDF or any other hosted file. If it's an MP3 or video, free services like Dropbox or Google Drive work well.

Step two accomplished! Now, Suzy moves on to step three, offering a free 30-minute call to those who've shown interest. She uses Calendly to schedule these calls and syncs it with her phone calendar for easy management. After the call, she can send them PayPal payment links to convert them into clients.

With that done, Suzy moves into the delivery phase. She'll create a YouTube channel with unlisted links, organising the content week by week in a PDF. She'll send this PDF along with Zoom call links to her clients using MailerLite's email sequences, which can be set up automatically or manually if necessary.

That's it—mission accomplished! Suzy has effectively utilised free technology to run her business smoothly, from social media to MailerLite, Calendly, Zoom, PayPal, and YouTube. This level one tech stack is perfect for starting out and doesn't require any costly upgrades.

Level 2 tech stack

In this section, we'll explore a more sophisticated tech stack for your website. I'll walk you through two types of tech stack, each with its own benefits. Let's begin with Emma, who wants to have her own website, let's call it "emmacoaching.com."

To start, Emma needs to buy a domain, which she has already done. She registered her domain with a hosting service called SiteGround, a brilliant option for hosting websites. Think of it like buying cloud space to store your website. The cost is around £6 per month for one website.

Emma chooses to build her website using WordPress.org, which is a free and open-source software for building websites. There are other website builders like Wix, but WordPress is simple to use and has easy drag-and-drop builders. If you can create a PowerPoint, building a WordPress website will feel familiar. WordPress.org is free (unlike Wordpress.com, to be clear), so you won't need to pay a monthly fee like with some other website builders.

If Emma prefers not to build the website herself, she can hire someone to do it. There are options to find web developers on platforms like Fiverr, where you can get a basic but decent website created for around £100-£150. Do be careful to read reviews and see how well the seller communicates with you before you opt to buy from them. The other option is to ask people, you know and trust, for web developer recommendations, but you can expect to pay a lot more that way.

Once her WordPress website is set up, she can start using plugins to enhance its functionality. One important plugin is a learning management system such as LearnDash, which allows her to deliver courses within her website. It costs around £100 per year, but some developers might include it for free when building your site.

For hosting video content, Emma can choose between Canva, Vimeo and YouTube. Vimeo offers more control and a slicker experience for online courses. It costs around £6 per month, while YouTube is free.

Emma can also use Mailerlite for sending reminders and updates to her course participants. The overall cost for this tech stack includes the domain (£10 per year), hosting on SiteGround (£5-6 per month), and LearnDash plugin (£100 per year). Optionally, Vimeo costs around £6 per month.

Remember, if this feels like too much, just think about what you want to achieve in the next few months. Don't feel like you must have a website to get started with your business - in fact, I'd argue that it should come later down the line. Get started with the free stuff, and don't get bogged down in website building in the beginning.

If the perfectionist in you won't let you move forward without one, there are easier, off-the-peg options like Teachable and Kajabi which come with a monthly subscription fee but you can get up-and-running in a day or so.

Filming your course

Whichever tech stack you opt for, you'll still need to consider how to put together and film your course.

You'll need to decide how you want to present your course—using Canva, PowerPoint, Google Slides, or Keynote. Personally, I use Google Slides but many of my clients love using Canva for everything.

There are different presentation options: face to camera,

screen recording, or a mix of both. I prefer screen recording because it allows me to focus on the content without worrying about my appearance.

For screen recording, I recommend using either Canva or Vimeo. Vimeo is my personal favourite as it allows both screen recording and easy hosting of videos, which saves time compared with having to upload everything to YouTube.

Once you've chosen your method, create your first lesson or welcome video. You can start with a simple video and improve later. Remember, there's no right or wrong way to do it; choose what suits you best.

Label your videos clearly with a numbering system like "Module 1, Video 1" or "Onboarding 1, Onboarding 2." This will make organising and sharing your content easier later on.

Don't worry about perfection; you can always redo and improve your videos later. Remember, taking the first step is the most crucial part. You're on your way to creating an amazing course!

Your marketing toolkit

Now we'll dive into selling your course or programme. Yes, that's right - we're going to sell your programme before you have even created it! Trust me, this is the best way. Stick with me and you'll see why!

We've already discussed our ideal client and marketing, so let's revisit the basics and develop a strategy along with some content for selling your course to the right people.

In this overview, we'll explore social media strategies for different platforms like Instagram, Facebook and LinkedIn. We won't use all of them; instead, we'll identify the best one for you. We'll also discuss the importance of having a Facebook business page and creating a group, but we'll decide if that's suitable for you later.

Sharing testimonials is one of the best ways to build trust with your audience. Think about anyone who you've taught in the past, no matter how long ago it was. Can you reach out to them and ask for a few words or even a video testimonial about their experience with you? These testimonials can inspire other potential customers to work with you.

Now, regarding social media, we won't overwhelm ourselves by being on every platform. Instead, we'll focus on one or two that align with your target audience. For instance, if you want to teach kids with dyslexia, you might find them in Facebook groups dedicated to parents of dyslexic children.

We want to be super focused on our content and avoid spreading ourselves too thinly across multiple platforms. So, let's figure out what platform suits your business best.

To create content, we'll refer back to our ideal client notes from chapter 13. You can mind-map ideas around their pain points and dreams for posts using this. This preparation will make content creation much easier and boost your confidence. You can even leverage Artificial Intelligence tools such as Chat GTP to help turn your copy into posts, blogs and emails.

Build your marketing strategy

Let's create an overview of your marketing strategy. Your marketing is all about connecting with your ideal students (and / or their parents), sharing your knowledge, and making offers. It may trigger some resistance when we talk about being visible to friends, colleagues, or others. However, unless you are already a social media enthusiast, you might need some time to adjust your mindset around this (revert back to the chapter on FEAR)!

Now, let's dive into how we're going to implement this strategy. First, you'll set up your profile on a specific social media platform. It doesn't really matter which platform you choose; the same principles apply. Your profile should focus on your ideal client, outlining how you can help them achieve their goals.

Soon, we'll discuss using an existing profile, like your personal Facebook profile, which can be an efficient strategy for getting clients. However, it may not be suitable for everyone, and I'll explain the pros and cons.

Once you've set up your profile, the next step is to join groups where your ideal clients hang out. Observe and like posts, and engage in conversations by answering questions and showing your expertise. Keep a spreadsheet to track the individuals who engage with you and show interest in what you offer.

When you notice potential clients, offer to connect with them on the platform. Start a conversation to build a relationship. After some back-and-forth, you can introduce your lead magnet, a helpful resource related to their interests or struggles. Eventually, you can offer a free call to discuss their challenges and how you can help them.

Most customers need about five to ten touch points before they feel comfortable enough to become a client. Keep track of your interactions with potential clients in your spreadsheet and follow up with them regularly.

Now, I want to address any resistance you might have towards being visible on social media. Write down all your worries and concerns about this. You might be worried about old connections seeing your content or colleagues discovering your online presence. Address each point one by one, and if necessary, declutter your connections. Remember, fear stands in the way of progress, and it's essential to face it.

I believe you can overcome any apprehensions and successfully implement your marketing strategy. I've got your back, and I'll be with you every step of the way. You can do this! Let's move forward together.

Using your Facebook profile

Now, we'll discuss the benefits of using your actual Facebook profile instead of a business page. Business pages have seen a decrease in organic reach over the years, making it challenging to get your posts seen, even by those who like your page. It's essential to understand organic posts, which are non-paid posts made on your business page, have lost their effectiveness.

While business pages do have their place, they are more suitable for running ads rather than starting out. It's best to establish your business using organic, free marketing methods first. Once your business is running smoothly, you can venture into Facebook ads.

It's essential to overcome any fear of visibility and declutter your Facebook profile of irrelevant connections. You don't have to be friends with everyone. Keep it focused on the people who matter and are relevant to your business.

Now, let's discuss the benefits of using your profile for business. With a personal profile, you have more control over your audience. You can add and engage with ideal clients, which is challenging with a business page. Your profile becomes your professional page, and it's essential to set it up accordingly with a clear headline that states who you help and how you help them.

Engagement is crucial. Connect with your ideal clients daily, join relevant conversations, and comment on posts that relate to your business. Regularly posting high-quality content, around three to five times a week, will also improve your visibility and engagement.

By leveraging your personal profile in this way, you can effectively engage with your audience and create a more relevant and trusting community for your business.

Joining Facebook groups to find your ICA

Whether you plan to use Facebook as your main lead generation source or not, starting by hanging out in relevant groups is essential. Remember, you can only join groups using your personal profile, not as a business page.

Even if you don't see Facebook as your long-term strategy, consider it an exercise in market research. Facebook groups are a treasure trove of potential ICAs, and you can find people to connect with and learn about their needs and problems.

To get started, join groups where you think your ideal clients hang out. Search for topic words and keywords related to their problems, dreams, and your offer. Utilise the information you gathered in unit one as a guide. When you find questions from your ideal clients, respond with high-value answers, not just simple offers to help.

Avoid posting direct links in other people's groups as it can come across as spammy. Instead, invite interested individuals to comment if they want a free guide or a call. Then, send them a personal message with the link. If they respond positively, you can even 'friend request' them to increase visibility.

Consider setting up your own Facebook group as well, but make sure to use qualifying questions to screen potential members and ensure they fit your ICA. However, remember to set boundaries to avoid feeling overwhelmed by group management.

When offering a call, make the outcome clear and qualify prospects by asking questions to ensure they are genuinely interested in your help. Follow up with prospects who show interest but might forget to take action. You can even use voice notes for a more personal touch.

In the next section, we'll explore whether setting up your own Facebook group is a good idea and how to manage it effectively. Remember to approach this process intentionally, with clear boundaries and expectations, to make it a successful part of your marketing strategy.

Running your own Facebook group

Let's take a look at running your own Facebook group as an option too. It might be a good business marketing strategy, but it's essential to figure out if it's the right fit for you.

With our BilinguaSing business, our group focus is on growing a vibrant community of parents interested in their children learning languages. We provide lots of free content, but we're careful not to overwhelm them.

Now, let's dive into the six reasons why you could consider creating your own Facebook group:

> **Bringing fans together**: Having all your top fans in one place allows you to create a sense of community and goodwill. You become their leader and expert, which boosts your authority.
>
> **Value-adding features**: Facebook groups offer excellent features like social learning, allowing you to provide valuable content, videos, and live sessions that benefit the members.
>
> **Market research**: You can use the group as a market research forum. Ask questions to understand their pain points better and tailor your offerings accordingly.
>
> **Valuable analytics**: The group's analytics provide insights into your audience's engagement, growth, and

top engagers, helping you refine your strategies.

Building bonds: The group fosters new friendships and bonds among members, all centred around your brand and shared interests.

Exclusivity: Offering occasional freebies or guides to your group makes members feel special and connected to you.

Managing a Facebook group requires some effort. Create clear rules and boundaries to set the tone and ensure courteous and respectful interactions. Engage consistently but avoid micromanaging, allowing members to initiate discussions.

Remember, it's crucial to be intentional and avoid falling into the trap of checking notifications all day. Set aside specific times to engage with the group and turn off notifications to stay in control.

Decide if running a Facebook group aligns with your goals and values. Take some time to journal your thoughts and feelings to make an informed decision.

Instagram

Now we'll go through some key points about Instagram to help you decide if it's the right platform for you. If you're considering Instagram, you'll be asked to choose between a personal, business, or creator profile. I highly recommend going with a business account as it offers more functionalities, such as analytics.

Instagram is all about visuals, so use fewer words and more pictures and videos, along with relevant hashtags. Your bio should focus on helping your audience and be concise, like "helping X people do X by X, Y, Z."

When it comes to posting, aim for one post per day on your grid and stories.

To grow your following, follow people who fit your target audience. Be consistent in adding new followers every day, and you'll likely see a return in followers as well. Engagement is essential, so leave meaningful comments on others' posts. Hashtags play a significant role on Instagram, so create a bank of relevant ones and include a few in each post.

I hope these insights help you decide if Instagram is right for you.

Is LinkedIn the one?

Next up, I want to help you see if LinkedIn could be a place for you. Personally, I love LinkedIn because when I started my business, I was searching for language teachers to join my network, and LinkedIn turned out to be the perfect platform for finding professionals by job title.

My primary focus has shifted slightly towards my 2-Hour Tutor coaching course, which is for all teachers and tutors. However, I still find LinkedIn an excellent place to connect with people who align with my coaching mission.

If you're looking to connect with specific types of people in certain professions, LinkedIn is perfect for that. But even if you are not that specific, you can still use LinkedIn to generate leads.

What does LinkedIn do? It helps us build authority around our profession and what we teach or coach about. It's an excellent platform for connecting with like-minded individuals who are more focused on work-related interactions. But remember, it's not a stuffy platform; it's a social network where being yourself is essential.

Setting up a business page on LinkedIn is a good idea, but the focus should be on your personal profile. Business pages have limited benefits, but you can add your logo and link it to your work and education section to give it a professional touch. However, it's better to focus on your personal page.

LinkedIn groups, though available, are not very effective for communication and connecting. They might help expand your network, but don't rely too much on them for meaningful interactions.

Your LinkedIn bio is crucial 'real estate'. As with the Instagram example, make sure it clearly conveys who you help and how you help them. Utilise relevant keywords to make it visually appealing.

Recommendations from connections are valuable; ask for personalised recommendations from people you've worked with, focusing on your current goals.

When reaching out to potential connections, aim for second-degree connections, and don't worry about sending personalised messages. Your headline and profile should clearly communicate your purpose, attracting the right people to your network.

Remember, LinkedIn can be an essential tool for your business, but it's crucial to stay authentic and focus on building meaningful connections with your ideal clients.

Scheduling your social media posts

Once you've selected your preferred social media platform(s), you can schedule your posts in advance, so you don't have to create new content every day. However, please note that personal profiles may not allow scheduling as they are meant for spontaneous and casual posts.

For business pages on Facebook and groups, scheduling is possible and highly beneficial. With a group, you can plan and schedule a month's or a week's worth of content in one go, ensuring that regular posts go out without the need for constant manual posting. It's a genius time-saving approach!

In the upcoming chapters, we'll dive into content plans. This will help you plan your posts for the entire month, so you can simply schedule and post them in advance.

For scheduling your posts, consider using cross-posting software like Hootsuite, Buffer, or my personal favourite - SocialBee. Hootsuite is beginner-friendly and free for up to three platforms. If you're using only one platform, you can utilise the built-in scheduling feature provided by the platform itself.

When using multiple social media platforms, be mindful of how much time you spend on them. Consider allocating a specific time each day for social media activities and stick to it to avoid getting lost in constant checking and engagement.

To recap, make a decision based on your preferences and needs. Do some research, and if you are comfortable with a particular platform or software, start posting right away. Don't overthink it or strive for perfection; just get going and begin building connections with your target audience.

There are some important rules for social media, which apply no matter what platform you choose. Avoid chasing random likes and followers. It might feel good to look popular, but it's essential to have an audience genuinely interested in what you offer. Quality over quantity is crucial. Engaged followers are more valuable than a large, disinterested following.

Next, adapt your content to the platform you're using. Each platform has its unique characteristics, and your content should match those. Avoid linking to external sites within your posts, as platforms prefer users to stay within their ecosystem. You can add links in the comments instead.

Engagement is key. If you want people to engage with your content, you need to engage with them first. Take time to interact with your audience, respond to comments, and show appreciation for their engagement.

Now, let's move on to creating clever content. First, put yourself in your audience's shoes and address the problems they face. Think about their pain points and what they need to know. Don't just talk about your business; provide valuable insights and solutions to their challenges.

When posting, maintain a balance. Only about 10% of your content should be direct sales posts, where you explicitly promote your products or services. Approximately 20% can be indirect sales posts, such as testimonials or success stories. The remaining 70% should focus on sharing valuable information and helping your audience.

Building a social media presence takes time and consistency. Be patient and committed to engaging with your audience, and the results will follow.

Focus on engaging with your audience, providing valuable content that addresses their needs, and maintaining a balanced approach to sales posts. By following these guidelines, you'll create a meaningful and effective social media strategy.

You want your audience to see you as a knowledge hub, the go-to channel to find valuable resources to help them with their problems. Share your teaching ethos to let them know if you're the right fit for them or their child.

If you offer more than one course or type of offering, avoid posting about them simultaneously. Focus on one thing at a time to avoid confusion.

In your posts, show your personality. Decide how much you want to reveal about yourself, whether it's family-related or more focused on you.

You can share short stories, freebies, resources, and quick-fix videos related to your expertise. Testimonials are valuable, even if they don't mention your current offering. Request testimonials from clients and display them as social proof.

- Ask questions to engage your audience and do market research. Quick tips and inspirational quotes related to your teaching approach work well.
- Remember to introduce yourself occasionally, especially for new followers who missed your earlier posts.
- Don't shy away from making offers about your programme to your audience; it's about providing a solution to their needs.

Creating content templates can be helpful, ensuring you have a bank of posts to reuse and adapt over time. Trello is a great app for managing social media content on the go.

Templates can include inspirational posts, personal stories, introductions to who you are, questions, success stories, testimonials, and more. These content categories are valuable and can be recycled, saving you time and effort.

Remember, social media content tends to have a short lifespan, so it's fine to create 'evergreen' posts that you can use repeatedly.

Find the method for creating and storing post ideas that works best for you and see if you can create a month's worth of content. Enjoy the process and happy posting!

Set yourself a challenge

Now you're in an amazing position. You have a good idea of your audience and what you're offering. You've got content ideas and a platform to promote yourself.

Now, let's take it up a notch with a 30-day challenge: get 100 leads. I challenge you to deliver a signature talk, a mini training session, or a free coaching/consultation session. The goal is to offer it to people who might be interested in your services.

To reach a larger audience, consider hosting the session online and invite people from other people's audiences to attend. Think about the Facebook groups you're part of and other communities where you could offer this valuable content.

Approach potential partners or groups and ask if they'd be interested in having you provide a bonus session for their audience. Some might not be open to it, but many will be if you're not offering the exact same thing.

Once you've refined your mini workshop, you can use it repeatedly to attract new clients.

Start by listing 10 places or people you can approach to offer your free signature talk. Prioritise them based on potential impact. It's often best to start with smaller groups to build your confidence.

It doesn't have to be complicated and you can reuse your talk in front of different audiences, making it a powerful way to get lots of leads at once.

While this method is effective, don't forget to also get leads from your social media presence. Combining both approaches will boost your audience, and when you're ready to pitch your programme, you'll have a warm audience that's more likely to respond positively.

Chapter 17

The non-salesy seller mindset

I know the mere mention of "sales" can make us cringe, fearing sleazy tactics or feeling like pushy salespeople. But let's set that aside for now.

The first thing I want you to do is forget everything you thought you knew about sales. Picture all those negative thoughts as items in a backpack and simply toss it off a cliff (safely, of course!). Selling, when done right, is just about sharing what you know and making offers.

Remember, marketing and sales are different but interconnected. Good marketing sets the stage for natural sales. Now, taking that first step and putting ourselves out there can feel daunting, but let's reframe it as an exciting opportunity to shape our new future.

You might worry about pushing people to buy from you, but it's essential to let them know about your solutions. Think of it as a chance to positively change their lives. You have the authority and expertise to help your audience, even if there are others in the same field. Your unique perspective and approach make a difference.

When discussing your offer or programme, focus on the end result—the transformation you'll bring to their lives—rather than listing all the features. Help your potential customers envision how their lives will change after working with you. Paint that picture for them, and they'll be more likely to take the journey with you.

It all starts with building relationships, sharing what you know, and serving your audience. Remember, you're not selling; you're solving problems and fulfilling their needs. Speak directly to what they want, and once they're on board, provide what they need. Avoid overwhelming them with details in the beginning.

By embracing these principles, you can create a compelling offer that resonates with your audience.

Remember, this is about helping others, and by doing so, you can become the go-to person in your niche. So, own your expertise, step into your authority, and keep showing up authentically for your audience. They are there because they want to learn from you.

These are all the end results, so we're painting a picture of that. Am I going to get excited by eight weeks of lessons, worksheets, and zoom calls? I'm a bit of a language nerd, so I probably would get a bit excited about that, but I would get far more excited about what's on the other side of the eight weeks. That's what we're talking about here: what do they want out of it at the end, and then what's your offer? How are you going to talk around your offer to bridge the gap between wanting and needing?

As you construct your offer, steer clear of expert language, education jargon, and acronyms. Your focus will be on speaking their language, ensuring a stronger connection and a more genuine experience, free from any 'salesy' vibes. With all the groundwork completed around your ideal client and offer, the result should feel aligned, satisfying and authentic.

I genuinely want this for you - it's within your reach, but remember, you must take the initiative to make it happen. Do you crave the freedom and control to shape your own destiny? Keep that vision alive. Remember, your authenticity will naturally draw like-minded individuals towards you. Embrace your expertise when answering questions or engaging with potential clients online, and confidently invite them to take the next step by joining you on a call. Seize the opportunity!

Discovery calls

I'm going to share my whole process for running sales calls (or discovery calls, as I prefer to call them) with teachers who are interested in joining the 2-Hour Tutor programme.

I've fine-tuned this process over the years, reducing it from over an hour to just 20 minutes. I understand that no one wants to spend their whole week on sales calls. So, let's aim for efficiency.

When I start the call, I take charge and set the scene, making it clear that we have 20 minutes to gain clarity on your current situation and what you'd like to achieve. It's essential for me to understand why you reached out to me, what you're looking for, and if I'm the right fit to help you.

Next, I'll go through your responses to the questions you provided when booking the call (these are hooked up to my calendly link), or any information you shared during the booking process. This helps me grasp where you currently stand and where you want to be.

Then, we'll identify any roadblocks that might be in your way. It could be financial, time-related, or other concerns. Addressing these roadblocks will help you gain confidence in moving forward.

Throughout the call, I want to connect with the emotions behind your desire for change. I want you to visualise what life will be like once your challenges are resolved. This emotional connection will guide your decision-making.

At the end of the call, I'll summarise our discussion, reiterating your current situation, desired outcome, and any roadblocks we identified. By this point, I'll be able to tell if I'm the right person to help you, and I'll let you know honestly.

If I feel I'm not the best fit, I'll recommend other options or resources that may be more suitable for you. My goal is to ensure you get the best support possible.

If I believe I can help you (and you tell me you'd actually like my help), you can take your time to consider the investment and any other details in the document I'll share with you after the call. Remember, this call is not about hard-selling; it's a coaching-style conversation to help you find the best solution.

If you adapt this approach with your prospects, you'll get a great response and you can start filling your programme with ideal-fit students who will rave about your programme, rather than saying 'yes' to anyone who you could help.

Convey the value of your programme

I really want to help you understand the true value of your skills and knowledge. By now, I hope you believe in the value you can provide to your students and that they understand the transformation they'll experience through your programme. Let's break down how you can build your offer so that this feels more tangible both to you and your students.

Here's an example: Imagine offering a one-year access to your eight-week coaching program or tuition course. This package could include recorded training videos, course content, and action-oriented worksheets. This alone, without any live support, could be valued at £500.

Now, let's assess the value of each additional element (let's assume you're running a 12-week programme):

- Your core, recorded programme could be valued at £500
- The weekly group coaching call package on Zoom could be valued at £400.
- One-to-one email and messaging support from you during the programme could be valued at £500.
- Additionally, you could include bonus access to your Facebook community or WhatsApp group as a bonus feature.

When you add up the value of all these elements, it comes to £1400. However, you want to offer all of this to your students for just £500. You can see that there's immense value in your programme, and you can confidently justify your price.

Feel free to adjust these elements and their values to suit

your preferences. You might choose to share all this information with your clients when making your offer, or you can keep it for your internal reference. The key is to know and have confidence in the features, benefits, and the transformation your programme brings.

I encourage you to do this exercise and list out all the features and their respective values. Once you've done that, you will truly know and believe the value of what you are offering your students.

If you think about it, 12 weeks of regular 1:1 tuition could cost roughly the same - but in reality it's likely to go on for much longer due to the tendency for this type of tuition to drift indefinitely.

Writing your course information or 'sales page'

Writing a 'sales page' is a great process because it prompts you to consider all the elements your clients might ask about, even the ones you hadn't thought of yet.

Everything you've done up to this point will be incredibly helpful for this phase.

First outline the problems they face, and how you relate to it. Outline your specific roadmap or blueprint for your program, detailing the transformation it offers and what the ideal client can expect. This helps paint a clear picture of what they can achieve and the results they'll experience.

Address any obstacles they might face and the problems they want to avoid in the future. Show them how your programme can change their lives for the better, instilling a sense of excitement and increased confidence.

You'll want to include some of the tangible features too:

- the name of your programme
- The logistics of delivery (length of time, videos, zoom calls etc)
- what your offer includes and its benefits
- any bonuses you want to offer
- whether you'll provide a guarantee to ease any customer concerns (by guarantee I don't mean guaranteed result for your students - we can only guarantee that we will do our part in helping them achieve their desired outcome. You may wish to consider a 'love it or leave it' guarantee in the first week, for example).
- The price, and whether you'll offer payment plans

Don't forget testimonials; they are powerful for showcasing the value of your programme. Also, anticipate and answer frequently asked questions (FAQs) that your ideal customers might have. Explain why your offer is unique and share your personal story, showing how you understand their pain points and why you're passionate about helping them.

By completing this, you'll have a valuable source of content you can draw from repeatedly. You can direct potential customers to it after a call or use it as a sales page on your website. It'll be a treasure trove of content that you can also use for social media and marketing.

Enjoy the process!

Chapter 18

Making it Happen

"Ok Ellie - so how am I going to find the time to do all of this?" you may be thinking. Let's discuss an essential word today: boundaries.

Successful people know the power of saying no. Warren Buffet, a self-made billionaire, emphasised that successful people say no to most requests that are made of them. Learning to say no and setting boundaries is crucial in various aspects of life, including your job or business, and personal relationships.

Our teaching job (whether past or present) is like any other relationship. How we respond to requests made of us has a significant impact on how others treat us. Many of us have been guilty of saying yes too often, just to please others or seek validation. This is a common struggle, and it's essential to recognise that only we can change it.

We must understand that a job is a two-way street, and we need to have firm boundaries. Otherwise, we end up being pushed around, drifting aimlessly without a clear direction. Take a moment to honestly reflect on your experiences and recognise where you might have let others take advantage of you.

To break free from being a people-pleaser, we need to establish an invisible bubble around ourselves. Think of it as your boundary, where no one should cross without your consent. Visualise people reaching into your bubble when they ask for your time or assistance. This will help you pause before reacting and give yourself time to assess if it aligns with your goals and priorities.

The most successful people have firm boundaries because they are selective with their time and energy. They consider if a request serves their goals and moves them closer to their desired outcomes. We, too, need to be more deliberate in evaluating how each request impacts our progress.

Having go-to phrases ready can be helpful when setting boundaries. For example, you can say, "I'd love to help, but I can't take on anything else right now," or "I'm not sure; let me check my schedule and get back to you." By using these phrases, you can be assertive yet polite in declining requests.

Setting boundaries will lead to positive changes in how others perceive and respect you. People will value your time and become more mindful of your needs. Remember, respecting yourself through clear boundaries will earn you more respect from others. Take charge of your time and make it work for you.

If you're transitioning from a teaching job to building your tuition business, establishing boundaries is crucial during this process. Treat your time like a valuable asset and use it wisely to achieve your goals. Be confident in saying no when necessary and avoid being a passive observer in your own life.

Journalling can be helpful in understanding what energises you and what drains your energy. Identify activities or tasks that bring you joy and fulfilment, and prioritise them in your schedule. Likewise, recognise situations or requests that deplete your energy, and learn to decline them gracefully.

Remember, it's okay to pause before responding to emails or requests. You don't have to react immediately. Give yourself time to assess if it aligns with your goals and whether you can accommodate it without compromising your priorities.

By setting boundaries, you gain control over your time and life. You will become more focused, productive, and fulfilled as you learn to say no when needed and prioritise what truly matters to you. This newfound empowerment will positively impact both your professional and personal relationships; it will allow you to schedule and protect the time you need to invest, in order to build your 2-Hour Tuition business.

If you really struggle with time management, The Steven Covey Time Management Matrix is a handy tool for teachers to sort their tasks by importance and urgency. It's like a to-do list on steroids!

It is based on the idea that not all tasks are equal in terms of urgency and importance. The matrix divides tasks into four boxes, allowing individuals to categorise their activities based on their significance and impact. The matrix is designed to help teachers (and anyone else) make better decisions about how to allocate their time and energy.

Here's a breakdown of the four quadrants:

> **Quadrant 1** - Urgent and Important: This quadrant includes any tasks that require immediate

attention. Examples include dealing with emergencies, handling urgent student issues, or delivering reports by the deadline. While these tasks cannot be completely avoided, effective planning and prevention strategies can reduce their occurrence. That said, if you are in a teaching role, most of your work sits in this box. I refer to this as the 'firefighting' box - many teachers exist in this mode most of the time, which explains why burnout is so prevalent in teaching (and perhaps why you are reading this book)!

Quadrant 2 - Not Urgent but Important: This quadrant contains tasks that are significant but do not require immediate attention. These tasks are vital for personal and professional growth and long-term success. Activities like curriculum development, developing systems and processes that reduce the need for firefighting, building relationships with students (marketing), and personal development fall into this quadrant. We should aim to spend increasingly more time in this quadrant to proactively address potential issues and improve our overall performance. The more time we spend in this box, the less time we need to spend in firefighting mode; and the 'upward spiral' I have referred to previously is set in motion.

Quadrant 3 - Urgent but Not Important: Tasks in this box are often distractions that demand immediate attention but do not contribute significantly to our goals. Examples include attending unnecessary meetings, dealing with interruptions, or attending to unimportant emails. We should aim to minimise the time spent in this quadrant to maintain focus on quadrant 2. This box will really test our boundaries!

Quadrant 4 - Not Urgent and Not Important: This box comprises time-wasting activities and distractions. Engaging in activities like excessive social media use, unproductive gossip, or random internet browsing should be minimised or eliminated as they have little to no positive impact on our future goals.

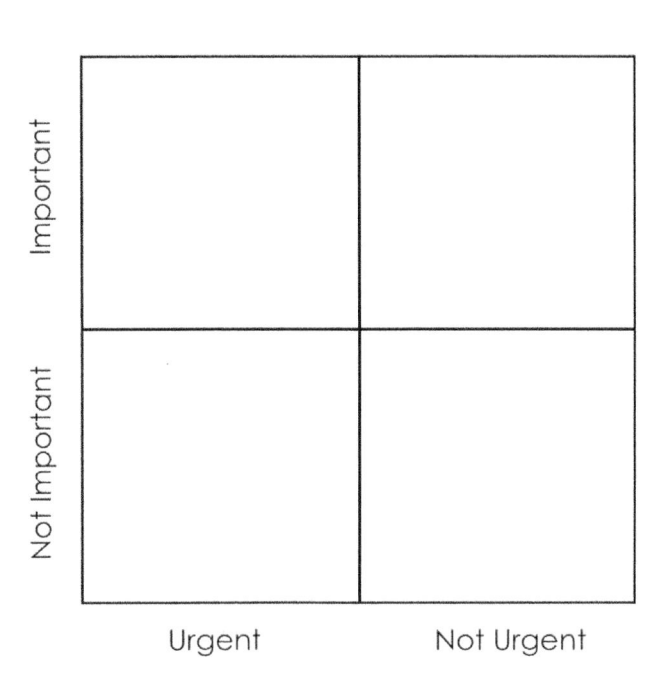

	Urgent	Not Urgent
Important		
Not Important		

Here's how it helps:

> **Prioritisation**: It helps us focus on what truly matters, like planning our business and building student relationships.

Stress Reduction: Less chaos, fewer last-minute fires to put out—hello work-life balance!

Better Planning: We become super planners, ready to handle anything that comes our way.

Time Efficiency: No more wasting time on silly distractions or unimportant stuff.

Personal Growth: We get to grow professionally and stay motivated.

New boundaries allow for new relationships

Now that you have identified some areas where you can free up more time, let's explore the concept of joint ventures, which are positive partnerships with other tutors and businesses in our niche but not direct competitors.

Back in 2013, when I started my language business, BilinguaSing; I formed a joint venture with a baby swim instructor named Jody. We both served the same market, new mums, and wanted to expand our reach without competition. So, we offered each other support and bonuses for our clients. For instance, I promoted her swim lessons to my customers, and she did the same for me, resulting in referrals for both of us.

Joint ventures are sometimes referred to as affiliate partnerships, where two businesses collaborate to grow each other's brand. It's a win-win situation. You can reach out to potential partners and offer something valuable to their audience, like giving a talk or a free resource (hello lead magnet)!

If they are willing to promote you, you can reward them with a percentage of the sales or other benefits.

Remember, joint ventures are excellent for positioning your authority and building trust with your audience. These partners can act as advocates, spreading your brand's reputation, and you can do the same for them. However, ensure that your values align with theirs before collaborating.

To start, make a list of potential partners you could reach out to and discuss mutually beneficial opportunities. This approach can be a game-changer for growing your business quickly and effectively.

Final words

Looking back to when you first picked up this book, did you know how to build a business or what an Ideal Client Avatar (ICA) meant? How to define an ideal client? How to create a package instead of hourly rates?

We now understand the importance of having a niche. Most of us, myself included, used to think anyone willing to pay was an ideal customer, but now we know better.

We've learned about marketing, writing effective sales copy, and managing our online presence. We know how to write sales pages and design a killer programme. We've become more financially savvy, creating equations that suit our needs and lifestyle.

I know you might still be working in a teaching job while reading this book, or maybe you are stacked with hours of 1:1 tuition; and it's challenging. But if you keep going and commit to this process, you'll get there. Your chances of success will be far greater, of course, if you seek out a support structure that will take you all the way.

While it is true that much of the knowledge shared here can be found for free on platforms like YouTube and Google, the reason why not all teachers and tutors are solely relying on these resources is simple: they require more than just information to achieve outstanding results.

This is where my full coaching programme, the 2-Hour Tutor comes into play, offering personalised help to overcome the various obstacles that may arise when implementing the theories and concepts discussed in the book. With my programme, you will receive the individual attention and guidance you need to help coax out your fab ideas, and successfully apply this knowledge to your unique circumstances.

One key element that sets The 2-Hour Tutor programme apart is the support and camaraderie of our community. Instead of going it alone, you will connect with like-minded professionals, share experiences, and learn from one another. The power of a supportive network cannot be underestimated; it provides a sense of belonging and motivation that can be instrumental in achieving extraordinary outcomes. Additionally, we'll help you navigate blind spots – areas where you may lack awareness or understanding – ensuring nothing is missed and that you have my eyeballs on everything you create.

In the world of education, time is of the essence, and often, teachers and tutors face time constraints that hinder their ability to fully see things through. Given the intensity of the job, this is understandable but so frustrating!

My programme offers you gentle accountability, pushing you to take action promptly and efficiently, ultimately driving results faster than you could on your own. Moreover, we understand that the journey towards success will not always be smooth, and during moments of doubt or setback, our programme is designed to provide a supportive hand, picking you up when you're feeling down and motivating you to persevere.

We often pay tradespeople for their time and expertise without a second thought. Now, consider investing in yourself, in your future, in your happiness. This is an investment that will pay dividends beyond measure.

What sets our programme apart are the 'Intangibles' we provide. With the 2-Hour Tutor programme, you gain access to a wealth of materials, the opportunity for regular catch-ups with myself and the other coaches, a supportive teacher community in buddy groups, and tailored 1:1 feedback that addresses your unique needs. The list of benefits goes on and on.

In essence, our programme isn't just an expense; it's a priceless opportunity to transform your life, overcome challenges, and unlock your full potential. As all of our clients say, the value we offer far outweighs the investment required!

CASE STUDY

From Head of English to replacing her teacher salary – meet Charley Crystal.

Name: Charley Crystal

Business: Crystal Clear Education (English Tuition)

Website: crystalclearenglishtuition.com/

Problem: On maternity leave with 3rd baby, needing to replace salary without relying on loads of 1:1 tuition

Success: Started group programme and had first sale within weeks of joining the 2-hour tutor, and replaced her salary within 6 months. On target to exceed salary.

Before working with Ellie...

From a mum on maternity leave, to gaining 17 clients upon completion of the 2-hour tutor programme and then replacing her salary in just 6 months, meet Charley Crystal.

Charley was a secondary school English teacher and head of department. She found it increasingly difficult to balance her demanding job whilst raising a young family. Following the birth of her third child, her request to return on a part-time basis was denied so she started thinking of leaving teaching. This led her to investigate creating her own tuition business.

She reached out to us at the 2-Hour Tutor programme as she wanted a way to continue teaching but with more flexibility and control over her own schedule. She realised she could potentially replace her teacher's salary by creating her own, online group tuition business.

Fast forward 6 months...

The support and guidance provided by the 2-hour tutor coaching programme helped Charley to create her own niche group tuition business and market it effectively, supporting English language GCSE students to achieve a grade 7-9.

Charley loves being her own boss and is now able to maintain a better work-life balance for herself and her young family.

Building relationships and seeing her students make progress within her programme over time has been highly rewarding and she thoroughly enjoys helping her students increase their confidence with their GCSE English.

Her advice to other teachers in a similar position is to give the 2-hour tutor programme a try as there is ample support, and you can make a great return on your investment.

Wondering if the 2-Hour Tutor approach will work for you?

To be completely honest, I can't provide a definitive answer until we've had a conversation. If you're interested in exploring further, I encourage you to submit an application. You can do so by visiting **elliebakereducation.com/work-with-me/**. Once we receive your application and details, we will carefully review the information provided, and if we appear to be a good fit, we will invite you to the next stage.

We highly value the quality of our programme, and as such, our spots are limited. However, rest assured that if we find that we're not the right fit for you, we will be honest about it and gladly refer you to another resource that we believe may better suit your needs. So, don't hesitate to submit your application – you have nothing to lose. We are committed to ensuring that you receive the best possible support and guidance on your journey, even if it means recommending an alternative option outside of our programme. Your growth and success are our top priorities, and we want to see you thrive in the most suitable environment. Apply now, and let's explore the possibilities together.

Remember, success is not a linear path; it's a journey filled with challenges and setbacks that ultimately lead to growth. Embrace the hurdles and keep moving forward. You don't need to have all the answers; just take one step each day, and you'll make progress. As a teacher, you possess unique talents that make you a superhero in your own right, so don't let doubt hold you back. Be true to yourself, and don't worry about what others think; focus on your growth and stay committed to your worth and the outcomes you can deliver.

As you embark on this exciting journey, remember how far you've already come. I am grateful that we found each other, and I hope this book has played a meaningful role in helping you create an aligned and joyful group tuition business. Even as you move forward, always trust in yourself and the process you've learned here. Take one step at a time, staying present, and avoiding overwhelm. Your curiosity, energy, and trust in yourself will pave the way to a fulfilling life.

Thank you for being my reader and investing in your growth. Remember that reviews can be a powerful way to share your experience and help others trust in the value of this book.

I'd love to hear your thoughts and stay connected beyond this book, so feel free to reach out via your preferred social platform or email. Let's continue to learn and grow together!

Thank you!

A poem that says it all, I think. I hope you find something here you can take with you on your journey.

The Road Not Taken
By Robert Frost

Two roads diverged in a yellow wood,
And sorry I could not travel both
And be one traveller, long I stood
And looked down one as far as I could
To where it bent in the undergrowth;

Then took the other, as just as fair,
And having perhaps the better claim,
Because it was grassy and wanted wear;
Though as for that the passing there
Had worn them really about the same,

And both that morning equally lay
In leaves no step had trodden black.
Oh, I kept the first for another day!
Yet knowing how way leads on to way,
I doubted if I should ever come back.

I shall be telling this with a sigh
Somewhere ages and ages hence:
Two roads diverged in a wood, and I—
I took the one less travelled by,
And that has made all the difference.

Bibliography

1. Covey, Stephen. (2020) *The 7 Habits of Highly Effective People. Simon and Schuster.*
2. DFE School workforce report. (2022) *https://explore-education-statistics.service.gov.uk/find-statistics/school-workforce-in-england/2022*
3. Duffield-Thomas, D. (2020). Chillpreneur. Hay House Business.
4. Frost, Robert. *The Road Not Taken (2010). Big Fish Publishing.*
5. Hendricks, Gay. *The Big Leap. (2009) Harperone*
6. Ramsey, Kane. (As quoted) "Practice makes permanent."
7. Rizzo, Steve. (As quoted) "Tell the big mouth inside your head to shut up."
8. Robbins, Tony. *Unleash the Power Within. (2020). Personal Coaching to Transform Your Life. Simon & Schuster Audio*

About the author

Ellie Baker is a certified Business and Life Coach with more than a decade of experience in coaching teachers to be education business owners. Prior to starting her first business (the children's language class franchise network, BilinguaSing), she was an MFL teacher in the UK education system for 10 years. During this time, she held numerous roles, including Head of Department, in a variety of educational settings including an 11-16 mixed comprehensive in Pontefract; a private girls school in Ascot, a grammar school in Slough, and several Middle and Primary schools in Windsor.

She has won a number of awards for business, including Family Business of the Year and Business Growth of the Year.

Ellie is lead coach in her programme The 2-Hour Tutor, where she helps teachers and tutors swap the 60-hour workweek for a 2 hour-a-week tuition business. She is also the CEO of BilinguaSing, where she continues to grow and develop her franchise network while supporting her franchisees to thrive in their businesses.

She lives in Maidenhead with her husband and three children.

Acknowledgements

I am incredibly grateful to my dad, Terry Hill, whose own best-selling coaching book The Inspiration Code ignited the spark within me to embark on this writing journey. Thank you for showing me that we can create our own path in life.

To my dear sister, Mel. Your dedication as my right-hand person, best friend, and business partner over the past decade has been immeasurable. I couldn't have done this without you by my side, and I am forever grateful. We are the dream team!

To my wonderful mum, Barbara, for her belief in us and her boundless support and encouragement. Thank you for instilling in us the belief that anything is possible with determination and perseverance.

My deepest gratitude goes to my amazing husband, Gareth, and our three incredible children, Seren, George, and Owen. You are my reason for being, my sense of purpose. You keep me motivated to fight for a better education system, not just for you but for all individuals within it. Your love and support sustain me every day.

Special thanks to my editor, Nerys, whose saintly patience, and unmatched eye for detail have made this book a reality.

Finally, I extend my heartfelt appreciation to my BilinguaSing franchisees, my wonderful coaching clients and all of you, my readers. Your support and trust in my work mean the world to me, and I hope that this book will resonate with you and leave a positive impact on your lives.

With love,

Ellie x

Leave a review

www.elliebakereducation.com

2-HOUR Tutor Blueprint

Printed in Great Britain
by Amazon